Good Works Review

2017

Editor-in-Chief
Robert S. King

Associate Editors
Ruth Bavetta, David Chorlton, Sara Clancy, Joan Colby,
Mike James, Marie C. Lecrivain, Rachel L. MacAulay

Production Editor
Diane Kistner

For More Information
www.goodworksreview.futurecycle.org

A Good Works Project of FutureCycle Press
www.futurecycle.org

Cover photo, "Fired Up" (U.S. Air National Guard photo/Staff Sgt. William Hopper); Cover and interior book design by Diane Kistner; PT Serif text with Macondo titling

Published by Good Works Review (a division of FutureCycle Press)
Athens, Georgia, USA

ISSN (applied; formerly 2376-9920)
ISBN 978-1-942371-90-8

Welcome to Good Works Review

Good Works Review is a Good Works project of FutureCycle Press. Introduced in 2013, these projects are altruistic collaborations of creative souls (like us) willing to give of their time, talents, and any profits to help improve our world. They have no source of monetary funding other than occasional sales of *American Society: What Poets See,* our first Good Works project.

With *Good Works Review,* we give struggling authors a way to submit their work without the necessary evil of reading fees, and all proceeds from sales are donated to charity. For this reason, the press gives contributors a Kindle edition of the issue in which their work appears upon publication, although on written request contributors can ask for a rebate on their paperback purchase. Clearly, the more copies purchased at full price, the more we can donate to worthy causes. To date (2017), FutureCycle Press has given an aggregate of several thousand dollars to the Malala Fund, Friends of the Earth, and Action Against Hunger for sales of *Malala: Poems for Malala Yousafzai, Weatherings,* and *Kentucky Review.* The ACLU is the beneficiary of all proceeds from *Good Works Review.*

To find out more or submit your work, visit www.goodworksreview.futurecycle.org.

Fiction

Poetry

Essays

Fiction

"Arches," photography by Thomas Gillaspy

Dave Barrett

Purgatory

Ben Ailing waits. He sits alone in the bar of his restaurant, the El Sombrero, at four in the morning, going over receipts from last night's bar ring-up, checking percentages, circling double ring-ups, counting the number of times the till was opened without a bill of sale.

"Twenty-seven times! Christ..."

Ben pushes the receipts away in disgust. He takes off his wife's reading glasses and places them on top of the string of receipts to keep them from snaking over into the undrained sink in back of the bar.

One more year.

Every year, for the last seven years, Ben and his wife, Myra, have been saying this. Every year they tell each other that this year will be their last. And every year they change their minds, put up with the lousy help and marathon hours, and go another round.

Ben Ailing lights up another Marlboro, and drinks from his cup of cold coffee with a shot of Bailey's Irish Cream in it. There are three watches on Ben's left wrist; all pawned off on him for an early morning drink. All broken. But they have good, solid steel hands (maybe even some gold in one of them, Ben thinks). Just in need of a little repair. He's been trying to pawn them back on his customers for two weeks now. So far, no takers.

Ben takes another drag from his cigarette, another sip of cold coffee. The bar is as quiet as a cocoon. The white stucco walls are yellowed with smoke, the piñatas hang - ing from the ceiling dull and fuzzy with dust. The only sound in the building—his building (the restaurant and the butcher shop out back taking up a quarter block of prime downtown Republic real estate)—is the occasional whirr of the ice machine downstairs and falling chinks of ice.

Ben Ailing is alone, abandoned by his family; excommunicated from a world he no longer understands, let alone recognizes. His wife, Myra, works fifteen-hour days here at the Sombrero. She says she works these long hours to keep their business afloat. But Ben knows the real reason—to keep away from him. And he doesn't blame her: their marriage fractured twenty, thirty years ago, when Ben started running around, back in San Francisco, where he made his mark buying and selling California real estate during the boom years of the '70s and early '80s, before they sold all their holdings (and missed the bigger '90s boom to come) to patch up their marriage, make a fresh start.

His boys—Will, Jerry, and Ben, Jr.—have abandoned him also. They want nothing to do with the restaurant. They flit in and out of town a month or two at a time, with their longhaired friends and vans broken down in his driveway. They work at the Sombrero just long enough to get monies together for their next big fiasco. Nashville. New York City. Chiapas, Mexico. His eldest son, Will, quotes Karl Marx and Henry George on the evils of private property, the ruin of unchecked Capitalism, the corruption of Man. Jerry, Ben's youngest, a pot-smoking guitarist, blames his inability to sell his songs on the bad Karma coming down on him for the sins of his father. Ben, Jr.—his middle boy—is the lone capitalist in this anarchical brood. But he is too easy a take, with his classic cars and cocaine habit and long string of debts. He wants all the goodies, but wants them all now, will suffer no restraints.

Ben's gaze shifts to the Budweiser Clydesdale display case atop the register. He's keying on the white plastic flakes the Clydesdales tramp across. Like the snowflakes in the shake-up universes Ben used to buy his boys—until he discovered they were using them for batting practice. (Little bastards! Smashed everything he ever gave them. Still do.) He's thinking of winter and his Canadian childhood. Deep in the belly of the Great Depression. His parents, Irish immigrants, ten children, his daddy's corner grocery store burning down. No insurance. His fifty-five-year-old Daddy out-of-work, out-of-luck, selling eggs and produce on a down Winnipeg street corner to pay the rent on their five acres and ramshackle house, $11 a month.

Ben's thinking of his earliest childhood memory. He's three or four years old. The whole family gathered round a big pot-bellied stove on a winter night. No TV. No radio. Bricks on the stove to warm their feet in bed. Daddy sitting quiet on his rocker, reading. Mama mending clothes. Ben and his nine siblings trying to avoid their Mama's wicked hand. Their only entertainment the howl of the blizzard outside, rattling the storm windows, seeping in through the cracks in the walls like water through a sieve.

And here it is: a brother taking him by the hand, leading him out from the circle of warmth. The bare wood floor cold through his threadbare socks. Then being lifted up, the sleeve of his brother's shirt wiping the frost from a window, making a porthole to see out of.

"Look, Ben! Wolves!"

There, thirty feet away. Great big gray ones. A dozen or more. Shivering in the snow. Going through the garden compost heap. Ribs on 'em like his Mama's washer board, showing right through the skin and fur. Bone white. Terrible.

The wolf at the door.

This is something Ben's boys have never seen, never will in all their travels. They'll never know what it's like to be so hungry a child must steal to fill his belly, beg neighbor women for bites to eat, see their Daddy bawl like a baby because he cannot feed his family.

But Ben does not suffer them this. He takes pride in their weakness, envies their gullibility. They are young. Forever young. They're out to make the world a better place. Save the planet. And Ben takes his hat off to them for it. But Ben knows what they're really up to: chasing rainbows.

His boys have heard all his stories and have been poisoned by them. Ben Ailing out on his own at 13. First with the Canadian National Circus, taking photos of couples in old-fashioned draped picture booths, keeping the freaks and fairies at bay, spreading his seed in a dozen farmer's wives and daughters from Newfoundland to British Columbia. Later laying track for the Canadian Pacific Railroad in the Yukon Territories. Ben Ailing boxcar rider, tree top logger, hod carrier and bare-knuckle boxer. His boys think they'll find that same something he found. And eventually, they'll discover what he discovered. Nothing. No Peace. No rest. No gold at the end of any of their rainbows either.

Youth. He had it too, strong as them. It drove him crazy most his life, made it hard for him to settle on anything less than everything, made him cheat on his good wife, made him beat on his good boys.

But now Ben's youth is over. Over. Finally, over. The face in the mirror behind the bar he doesn't recognize anymore. His black wavy hair is gray and thinning, his jaw shrinking so much he needs a new set of false teeth, his black Irish eyes—that once drove the girls in Toronto and Montreal wild—only make him look like a mean dog now. And Ben's glad for it. He's tired of his sinner's face, tired of the sinning. He smokes his last Marlboro down to its filter, stubs it, and then slowly peels the cellophane wrapper off another pack. Just biding his time. No longer waiting on better days. Fresh out of fresh starts. Just waiting. Simply waiting. Waiting for the punish-ment to come.

Gershon Ben-Avraham

Once Upon a Sabbath Afternoon

For the most part, Gittel was happy with Shmuel. He was not unhandsome. He worked hard. Most importantly, he loved her. He was not as tall as she would have liked, his hair was unruly, and sometimes he was too serious. Her parents had preferred Teivel Krantz, but Gittel preferred Shmuel.

For his part, Shmuel was *very* happy with Gittel. She was an excellent cook, and smart. Once he had seen her coax a kitten down from a tree with a piece of pickled herring tied to a string while all her friends had stood around sighing and wringing their hands. And—it must also be said—Gittel was pretty. In the end, however, what mattered most to Shmuel about Gittel was that Gittel...was Gittel.

Like all young couples starting out, Gittel and Shmuel encountered bumps along their road, but that they were traveling it together was a source of comfort to them. Every Friday night, Shmuel would come home from the Evening Prayer to a house filled with the aromas of Gittel's cooking, a table set in white, and two candles burning brightly. After dinner, when they went to bed, Shmuel, remembering what Rabbi Isaac had taught him, ensured the room was dark, and worked to create a mood of holiness, in case the Holy One, blessed be He, should grace their union with a child.

•••

Following Gittel and Shmuel's marriage, Rabbi Isaac suggested that Shmuel find a study partner. He recommended Teivel Krantz, who had recently become engaged. Sabbath afternoons, between the Afternoon and Evening prayers, Shmuel and Teivel learned together. Once, while they were studying Chapter 1 of *Ethics of the Fathers,* where it is written that one shouldn't talk overly much with women, even one's wife, Teivel asked Shmuel if he talked much with Gittel.

"No, not too much," Shmuel replied, uneasily, thinking of how often he enjoyed talking with Gittel, the sound of her voice, her laughter.

"You must be careful," Teivel said. "It says here that a man may inherit Gehinnom for this."

Shmuel was silent.

Walking home, Shmuel kept thinking about what Teivel had said. That evening he was quieter than usual.

"Cat got your tongue?" Gittel asked.

"No, I'm just thinking."

Gittel let Shmuel think all evening.

•••

For Rosh Hashanah, Shmuel wanted to buy Gittel a new shawl. To earn money for it, in addition to his work as caretaker of the community's cemetery, he worked as a woodcutter. He often arrived home exhausted, but imagining Gittel's happiness with a new shawl made the work bearable. One Sabbath, after the Morning Prayer, Shmuel came home, ate quickly, helped clear the table, then went straight to bed.

The bedroom door opened a crack. Gittel peeked in.

"Are you all right?" she asked, her dark hair hanging loosely around her face as she leaned into the bedroom.

"Yes, just a little tired."

"Shall I rub your head?" she asked, entering the room and closing the door behind her.

He wanted to say yes, but said no instead.

"I need to sleep," he said.

Gittel turned to go. Shmuel regretted his words.

"Gittel, I'm sorry. It *would* be nice."

Gittel fetched a blanket.

"We may need this," she said.

A cloud moved in front of the sun, and it began to rain.

•••

After the Evening Prayer, Shmuel approached Rabbi Isaac.

"Rabbi, I have a question."

"A big question, or a little question, Shmuel?"

"I'm not sure."

"Well...what is your question?"

Teivel Krantz walked up. Shmuel faltered.

"Uh...um..."

"I'm sorry Shmuel. I haven't much time now. I have to go to Rymanów tomorrow and need to prepare for my journey tonight. Come see me the day after tomorrow."

Shmuel promised himself not to be close with Gittel until after speaking with the rabbi.

He walked out into the night. The sky was filled with stars. The air was chilly, but not uncomfortable. The moon shone brightly over the fields. He heard night birds calling one another, and the stream, running alongside his road home, sang sweet melodies to him.

•••

On the appointed day, Shmuel went to Rabbi Isaac's house. The rabbi's wife answered the door.

"Is Rabbi in?" Shmuel asked.

"Yes, please come in. I'll tell him you're here."

Shmuel sat in the hallway. He heard doors opening and closing, and the murmur of voices. A quarter of an hour passed before the rabbi appeared.

"Sorry to keep you waiting, Shmuel. Let's go to my study."

In his study, the rabbi sat at his desk. Shmuel sat across from him.

"So, what is your question?"

"I'm not sure how to ask it," Shmuel said.

"So then, just ask it."

"Rabbi, I always try to do the things you taught me. I am grateful..."

"Shmuel, I know this. Please, just ask your question."

"Sabbath afternoon, I was with Gittel."

He paused, not sure how to continue.

"Shmuel, this is not a question."

Shmuel blushed.

"Was it all right for me to be with her in the afternoon?"

"Ah! I understand....It depends."

"Depends?"

"Yes, on what you were thinking."

"I...I forgot to think of Torah."

The rabbi folded his hands together on the table and looked at Shmuel.

"Shmuel, I believe you did remember."

"No. Rabbi, I..."

"When you walk along the river and hear it singing, or when resting from work raise your eyes to a grassy meadow, or at night see all the lights in the heavens, what are you thinking?"

"I'm thinking...how wonderful is the Master of the Universe."

"Exactly."

•••

Walking home, Shmuel thanked the Merciful One—for the rabbi, for covering the sun with a cloud, for the rain, but most of all, for Gittel.

And he began to sing.

Guy Biederman

Pink Fleece

He glimpsed the pink of her fleece coat through the trees from the porch of his cabin, a moving flash against brown trunks, green boughs, and grey sky. Who wore pink in the woods? A City Girl. Was she here with her boyfriend?

Luke returned to the postcard he was writing to Mary Beth.

Dear Sweetheart, it began.

It's what came out of his pen. But his eye told him it didn't feel right. Now it was on the Camp Emandal postcard he'd paid two dollars for, with a watercolor of a deer drinking down by the river and he thought, too late now—it's in ink. Kind of like the relationship. Damn metaphor. Damn ink. Damn pink fleece.

Truth was, they'd glued things back together with weekly $150 sessions. And no cracks showed. But would it hold water? That's what he wanted to know.

And that's what the therapist would not tell him.

The psychic, on the other hand, advised him in no uncertain terms he should appreciate what he had, not what he didn't have; that he needed to vacuum out his mind and stop thinking. Right. He liked her over the phone, a cat lady somewhere in Canada. But then she retired. How did a psychic retire? Could you turn off the visions?

One night at Smitty's, his pal Dodge went straight to the heart of the matter. "Luke, I've had a beer and I'll tell you the truth. Dude, you are your own worst enemy."

That brilliant analysis only cost him a Pliny the Elder. Well, two.

Luke went inside and filled a glass with mountain spring water from the tap. Took a sip. Walked down to camp. He played ping-pong with friendly strangers, attempted yoga with Leo, the rough-and-tumble watercolor instructor, tried to make a potholder out of fabric, decided to call it a welcome mat for one foot instead.

Saw no pink fleece in camp.

At twilight, he walked to the river. A pink sunset reflected in the fast-moving water. A deer appeared, eyed him tentatively, and took a sip.

Guy Biederman

Ape Man

I put on an ape suit and walk among the living so no one will know who I am. It does not go unnoticed. Six-year-old Petey notices right away and points as his mother picks him up and they scurry away to their Town & Country minivan. The mailman grins when he hands me my stack of bills along with a flyer for heater duct cleaning in July.

I go about my day. It gets hot wearing that suit. Amazing what one gets used to. Adaptability. I go to a conference of mascots. A Giant Chicken, a Statue of Liberty, a Sumo Wrestler, and a slender French Fry with a Short Fat Sausage...I'm thinking she can do better, the Fry, but who am I to judge?

We talk about our work. Cheering teams, working crowds, holding signs for free pizza and carpet cleaning solutions, and how one day, says a Pillsbury Doughboy knockoff, the people won't even notice you.

Yeah, they'll just take you for granted, says Sausage.

And that's a good thing, says Smokey.

And I can see that the room is filled with us. My tribe. Sweating inside these ridiculous suits. I feel exhilarated. Like I've come home. Like I can reinvent who I am, and strangely expose myself in disguise. I'm literally rising off my feet—walking on air three feet off the ground and the whole room looks at me.

The chant begins. "Here we go Ape Man, here we go."

And Rooster belts out a cock-a-doodle-do.

"Here we go Ape Man, here we go!" The chant takes hold, sweeps across the room. French Fry bobs wildly. Pillsbury somersaults into Sumo, who rolls him back to Panda, who, in his words, "is so dadgum sick of being hugged he could puke bamboo shoots which he hates but would gladly do if it would stop the ladies in curlers and the snotty nosed kids who think they are the first and only to find him cute, from conveying their affection."

So there.

So here.

I am evolving backwards. This feeling comes over me. I head for the door and they follow. We pour into the street, flood the sidewalks, this band of mascots, misfits, and miscreants. "Judge this," we cry with glee, pinching our fur, dancing with enlightenment, or at least the Light Bulbs—a set of six multi-colored who only work at Christmas but stay in their attire all year. And I see my future, as we walk across the crosswalk stopping traffic. It is nothing but authentic. A sweet Rabbit walks beside me. I hold her foot with my opposable thumb. Lucky.

Rachel Chalmers

The Heart on Pluto

I was late, and when I finally got to the speaking venue, Mark was waiting outside. Not good. Worse, he was wearing his Italian suit. He looked me up and down and said, "Really?" I was in combat boots, ripped jeans, and a hoodie.

"Lost track of time," I said.

"Shocker," he said. "Did you at least bring my speaking notes?" I handed over the index cards, which I'd written for him late the night before. "Thank fuck for small mercies," he said.

"You're welcome."

"Don't be a cunt."

"Not that there's anything wrong with cunts," I said.

"Agree to disagree," said Mark.

We registered and Mark went off to get hooked up with a microphone. I made a beeline for the bar. Most people were milling and networking. I'd rather die. I drank my free beer and caught the eye of a fifty-something man who looked almost as disgruntled as I felt. I raised an ironic glass to him and to my surprise, he winked. I sidled over.

"Like the wedding of a close friend you secretly can't stand," I said.

"Bat mitzvah for a King Charles Spaniel," he suggested.

"Fundraiser for a furry Burning Man camp."

"Landmark Forum graduation."

"Esalen reunion."

"No, that sounds rather fun."

"I knew I liked you," I said as we clinked glasses. "I'm Archie."

"Archibald?"

"Archimedes."

"Fancy!"

"Dad was an astronomer."

"Oh, was he? Anyone I know?"

"Not likely. Amateur. IBM sales-droid by day."

"And what do you do, Archie?"

"Kept man. You?"

"Planetary scientist."

"I bet you say that to all the boys."

"Maybe," he said, fishing out a business card that read: David Russell, PhD, NASA Ames.

"Oh, my God," I said. "You're a planetary scientist. Like Bobak."

"Yes. But he works on Mars, and I work on—"

"Christ, I hope you're going to say—"

"Pluto," we finished together. I put down my beer and unzipped my hoodie.

"Can't say it's ever worked this well before," he admitted.

I showed him my T-shirt, which said "I heart Pluto," except that the heart was a cartoon of the pink New Horizons image of Pluto with its southern hemisphere heart.

"Love your work," I said. "I mean it."

The corners of his eyes crinkled with pleasure. "Househusband, you said? Are you sure you're not underemployed?"

"Oh shit," I said. The staff were trying to herd us to the auditorium for Mark's talk. I made it to one of the last available seats. Mark scowled at me from the stage. Dr. Russell got the very last seat, which was next to mine.

Mark's talk was not great. It would've been better if he had done more prep, worked harder on his dissertation, been a stronger public speaker, or had a smaller sense of entitlement. I'm not being fair, but he did himself the much bigger injustice. He wasn't a stupid person. They don't give out doctorates in artificial intelligence for good citizenship. He was just very proud and very insecure.

After the Q&A without any audience questions, and the desultory applause, Dr. Russell and I made our way back through the crowds to the bar. Miracle of miracles, we found an unclaimed table. I was glad he seemed to want to stick around.

"Pluto," I said. "Rivers of nitrogen. Hit me."

"There's a water ocean under the heart."

"No way. Water how? It's so far away, and so cold."

"Well, it's slushy. But it's a rocky planet. Planetoid. Turns out there's enough geothermal there to keep it warm."

"And sustain life?"

"Oh yes," he said, deadpan. "We're sending a diplomatic mission next week. To steal their Death Star plans."

"Jerk," I said, laughing, and Mark chose that moment to walk by and drop the index cards in my lap. I stopped laughing.

"At least you're having a good night," said Mark.

"Mark, this is Dr. David Russell," I said.

"David, please."

That felt weird, but: "David, this is my husband, Mark."

"Archie and I have been talking about Pluto," said David.

"Oh God," said Mark, "don't let him turn on the bloody Syfy channel; it's impossible to turn it off again."

"A feature, not a bug," said David. "I work at NASA."

"Oh, do you? That'll be right up Archie's alley. Do you study Uranus?"

"It's pronounced Uranus, and no."

"Right, Pluto. So: planet or dwarf?" asked Mark. I'd known he would go there, but I winced anyway. It is exactly the least interesting question to ask about Pluto.

"I don't really pay attention to that kind of thing," said David. Mark wasn't listening. He was already looking over our shoulders to see who else in the room would be more help to his career.

"Oh, there's Barney," he said. "Come along, Archie."

"You go," I said. "I'll be another minute."

Mark gave me a look that felt like it should've burned holes in my skin, said "suit yourself," and walked away.

"It's a stressful night for him," I mumbled. I was blinking hard, because I choose not to be the kind of boy who cries in bars after marital spats.

"No need to apologize," said David. "Where were we? Oh yes, the ice. You know Pluto and Charon are tidally locked, right? And that the heart is on the anti-Charon side."

He talked about how the heart-shaped depression had enough mass to cause Pluto to wobble on its axis. Polar wandering, it's called. Earth has it too. He talked about how the likeliest cause was subsurface water. He was very interesting, and he talked long enough for me to get my shit together emotionally, so I liked him more than ever.

"I'll let you in on a little secret," I said. "I have an icy heart myself."

"Who among us doesn't?" asked David. We were well into our second beers at this point. "I've buried two husbands. I'm basically a black widow."

"God, I'm so sorry."

"Oh," he said, with a fluttery hand gesture, "this was in the late eighties, early nineties. AIDS War One. I rode dinosaurs to their steampunk funerals, and so on."

"A friend of mine failed retrovirals," I said, and winced. I never talked about him.

"AIDS War Two. I'm sorry. Tell me about him," said David.

I drained the rest of my beer. "Gonna need another drink," I said.

It's not even that there's that much to tell. It was the semester I spent in London. Mark and I had agreed we'd be open, but tell each other everything. Pete was in my class. He was cute and dreadlocked and fucking hilarious, and after one long night of drinking and dancing and cracking one another up with increasingly obscure jokes, I went back to his apartment and had the best sex of my life, repeatedly.

He made me pancakes the next morning, and it was all very delightful until I called Mark, as agreed, and Mark went nuclear, as not-agreed, and made me promise not to see Pete socially ever again. Since ours was a small and close-knit class, this put a crimp in my style. Since Pete's meds were already failing him, he was back in the hospital before the semester was out. He didn't graduate. I heard much later from mutual friends that he had died.

For whatever reason, I hadn't told anyone before. While I strive not to be the sort of boy who cries over marital spats, it turns out I can't be the sort of boy who talks about Pete without tears spilling out of my eyes. He deserved so much better, from life in general and from me in particular. I never even apologized.

David was somehow holding my hand. When I'd calmed down enough to hear him, he said gently: "You know, if a one-night stand of yours is sobbing over you, years after you died, you probably won at life."

I was hiccupping, because dignity. Mark was glaring at me from the other side of the room. "You're very kind," I said.

"Me? I'm just one more bitter old queer with a space robot," said David. "To a first approximation, we're all kind. No other way to survive. Don't lose my number, okay? I live in a big house above the Castro. It's full of lost boys."

"I'm not lost."

"In case you get lost."

"New Horizons?"

"New Horizons. Haven't you ever wanted to boldly go?"

I laughed. "Sure, why not," I said. "Make it so."

Joan Colby

The Ruins at Chichen Itza

Old Mr. Singleton labored along under the hot Mexican sun, with his head extended like a turtle's and his spine hunched beneath the invisible carapace of his heart trouble. His eyes had the inward-looking reptilian glaze that had characterized these last few years when age—heretofore held at bay by whacking tennis balls and pumping stationery bicycles—had overtaken him. He was approaching the Temple of the Warriors. Haltered with a Nikon, his bright yellow cardigan flopping loosely over a frame gone gaunt in one place and paunchy in another, he shuffled to the precipitous staircase and began making frames with his fingers, settling on angle, preparatory to setting the focus and aperture of the camera and lifting it to his squint.

His daughter Angela, a skinny crop-headed woman of 40, stepped briskly past, taking notes in a reporter's notepad.

"I'm going up," she said, pointing to the wide flight where tourists were hauling themselves by a length of chain to the parapet of the temple. Mr. Singleton didn't acknowledge this. He was blowing his breath out in the small toad bubbles that meant his angina was acting up.

Angela paused, "Did you take your pill?"

He glared at her vacantly. "A nitro. But I think it's my diverticulitis now." He fumbled at his leatherette camera case, which held assorted prescription vials, and found the one he was looking for.

For years, he had dreamed of this trip, since he was a boy actually, reading Prescott and pulsing with adventure, conquest, the secrets of the Maya. Now at last arrived, he was too late—unable to attend to anything but his body, that fascinator of age, seducing with its aches, twinges, and sudden amazing stabs that cored the dulling nerve, making him remember what it was to feel so acutely, and how immense the loss, poised in all his bones, would be.

"You don't look good," Angela said. But Mr. Singleton was aiming the camera now, trying to cram the entire astonishing edifice in the viewfinder. A tour group led by a dark, stocky man speaking rapid Spanish went past. To the left, another bunch; this one composed of English speakers. They huddled under a pepper tree, trying to determine from maps of the ruins whether they were looking at The Governor's Palace or The Nunnery. Angela knew it was neither, but refrained from going over to say so. You make a remark and the next thing some fat woman is telling you about her hysterectomy, her grandchild, her 30-year-old son's unfinished dissertation.

Instead, mastering her nervousness about heights, Angela marched to the pyramid and began to climb, angling back and forth, snakewise, as they had been instructed. She looked directly at the stair level with her eyes, knowing that a glance up or down could result in frozen panic like that Japanese girl this morning, coiled like a question mark halfway up, unable even to signal her plight. Finally, one of the guides had noticed and gone up to talk her down, step by step, showing her how to straddle the chain for security.

At the top, looking out across the scrubby Yucatan jungle, Angela wondered why it was important to climb every single pyramid. A flash of yellow below—her father moving over to the English tourists. Shading her eyes, Angela could see he'd put on the Panama hat bought from a street vendor in Merida. She wondered if the sun was getting to him.

On the ground again, she couldn't pick him out right away. There were several groups now touring the ruins, their big silver buses drinking the shade under a stand of the ubiquitous peppertrees.

There he was, unrecognizable for a moment, with the Panama creased and tilted to give a jaunty look to his dark, unlined face. His eyes, shiny and black as carved obsidian, were intent on a tall, big-boned woman with yellowy-white hair pulled back into a Scandinavian knot.

"The Spaniards named these temples according to their cultural viewpoint, largely defined by Catholicism," Mr. Singleton was pontificating, and the big Swede, who on closer inspection was nearing the 70 mark, looked suitably impressed.

He didn't spare Angela a glance as she strode up. The conquistador, she thought.

Two years later, standing at his deathbed, Angela watched her father's great fixed eye glare at the ceiling. The nurses said he couldn't see a thing, didn't know a thing, but that was difficult to believe. He'd been a man of powerful intellect, a compendium of ideas, notions of form and clarity. She recalled how he could go on about the qualities of light with a photographer's passion.

Dr. Oliphant explained that her father had been oxygen-deprived, so the brain damage he'd sustained would render him a vegetable if he ever did awaken. And he wouldn't. The respirator breathed for him.

"It's not a simple matter to disconnect once we've started the process," the doctor had explained. "In this state, the law requires a court order to disconnect a life-support system. Or the patient has to approve disconnection himself."

"How many patients on respirators can ask to be disconnected?" inquired Angela. The doctor closed his mouth and stared at her angrily.

"None of them, right?" she continued breezily. What a catch-22 situation. The state didn't recognize living wills either. There was a lot of money in keeping these old people alive. Medicare would pay. No wonder the country was going broke; Social

Security would be bankrupt by the time Angela or any of her generation hit retirement age.

The sight of her father trapped in his deathly flesh with that one malignant staring eye maddened her. Just that morning, she'd awoken to find a bird battering itself against her motel window. Again and again, it bombed the window, a brilliant kamikaze. She'd waved a blouse at it, trying to dissuade it from its suicidal mission. Rationally, though she knew the bird was attacking what it perceived as a rival—its own reflection—she could not vanquish the thought that it embodied her father's spirit demanding to be set free.

In the two years since their Mexico trip, Angela had not realized how severely his health had failed. There had been intervals of decline—a slight stroke, a seizure of some type that was never really diagnosed, maybe a lack of potassium, maybe an arterial spasm. From each assault of his body, her father had rallied, gathering his vital forces, regrouping, redefining the limits of his life. The daily tennis game denigrated to a jog, then a brisk walk, finally a slow one, at last a few steps down the catwalk of the condo using a walker. This final time, after he'd entered the hospital, he'd wept. That her father with his severe Spaniard's face should weep, appalled Angela. When she went to clean up the condo, a neighbor reported that her father's cat had run off. "Cats leave a house when death enters," the woman said.

She faced the doctor. "How much longer? Weeks? Months?" Visions of a nursing home, years of bedsores, tube feedings, rose before her.

"More like days," the doctor responded. "His kidneys are shot. We'll stop dialysis."

That faintly registered. Dialysis on a comatose man? But ever since her father had gone into arrest, nurses and doctors filling the room with their rigmarole, excluding Angela, she'd been incapable of thinking clearly. The one thing she knew was that he'd never wanted this. He'd demanded once that she refuse extraordinary measures on his behalf should it come to that. But they'd never asked her.

His heart pumped erratically across the monitor. "Doctor has ordered another EEG for this afternoon," the nurse said. "If it's flat, we might turn off the machine. It's hard on the family, I think." She lowered her voice confidingly. "I can't think why they put a man of your father's age and condition on the machines at all."

Angela was exhausted. Should she eat something? She stopped at the hospital cafeteria and sipped at a cup of coffee. The sky was white and blazing with the tropical sun. Outside the window, a tiny lizard scampered along the walk. A heaviness descend- ed on her as she rose and headed for the elevator. A young man and woman got in. With horror, Angela saw the man had no nose. A Band-Aid covered the place where his nose should have been. Its lack made his cheekbones and chin look angular, shoveled. His whole face looked scooped out. She felt sick and turned away. The young man's pale eyes followed her in disdain. The girl with him was equally young. She had her plump arm around his skinny hips. My God. What had happened, Angela wondered. An accident? Cancer? The elevator doors slid open and she stepped swiftly out.

Dr. Oliphant strode up to her with purpose. He came right up to her and halted. "Your father expired a few moments ago," he announced. The shock of it hit her, blinding as the Yucatan sun. This was the result of wanting the life-in-death existence of her father halted; the result was death. How could she have failed to realize that? Somehow, a frail flutter of hope had remained that he would, ever the conquistador, suddenly rise from his coma, unhook himself, take charge.

The only person who had ever loved her unconditionally with a severe intellectual love was gone from the world forever.

The doctor asked about an autopsy.

"No, for what purpose?" Angela said.

The doctor looked briefly annoyed. These fly-in relatives with their last-minute criticisms. Time to get down to business.

"You'll have to arrange for the removal."

Angela stared at him, puzzled.

"The mortician. I trust you know someone? Or the social worker can make a recommendation."

Of course, there would have to be a casket, burial, perhaps some type of memorial service? There were a few friends still mobile, though many of her father's business acquaintances were dead or confined to nursing homes.

When they were in the Yucatan, the guides had said the pyramids were places for worship, not tombs as in Egypt. But recently, Angela had read an article refuting that idea. Bones had been found in Mexican pyramids. But so little was known; even the language mostly a mystery. She had no one to talk to about this now. Her father was not a religious man. Would he have wanted cremation? Burial? A pyramid?

She thought of the tears that had rolled down her father's cheeks as he lay in the hospital bed a few weeks before. Struggling, he said, "I'm too emotional. I've always been too emotional."

Angela was astonished. Her father, Mr. Singleton, always a pinnacle of composure, stern, resolute. A man known for his ability to fix anything. Never one to give into feelings. A stoic. As she herself had, for so long, tried to be.

She began to sob. "Come, Ms. Singleton. Why don't you just rest in the waiting room for awhile?" the doctor said. "I'd like you to take a tranquilizer, it will get you through the next few hours. Is there anyone with you? Anyone to drive you?"

Angela shook her head. No one. She thought of the well of the sacrificial virgins. How the ancient priests had rubbed peppers into the victims' eyes to make them weep as a gift to Chac, god of rain. Tears pleased him. It seemed correct to weep for her father. Outside, the brilliant unforgiving sun shone relentlessly.

Zeke Jarvis

The Grieving Process

It shouldn't have been that hard to make the ribs look good. Even if they're not cow ribs, they're still ribs, so it seems like you should be able to just cook them, dump sauce on them, and put them on the table with some fries or mashed potatoes or something. With this being our last night of eating Dad, it seems like just smothering him in something from a jar and being done with it would be kind of appropriate. Instead, my mom takes tonight as an opportunity to break out an old cookbook that Dad got her. Something gourmet, which is more work for half the taste. Like the little green thing on our plate. I'm sure it was expensive, but I have no idea what it is. A mini pine tree, maybe? I'm not even going to sniff it.

To be fair, my mom's parents died together, in a car accident, where there wasn't much left of their bodies. So, when she was going through the grieving process, she never saw how to do things. You can understand why she can't get it right with our dad. But, still, there are some things that everyone knows. For instance, you do things like tacos or spaghetti, the things where the meat is the least important, during the first few days, when everything still tastes like ash. Especially if your loved one died from something like cancer, where you think that you can taste it in the meat, even though science tells you that that's impossible. Or maybe science doesn't tell you that; I guess I don't know if it's ever actually been studied or how you would study what cancer tastes like. Anyway, spaghetti and tacos and stuff like that distract you from what you're doing. Or you eat the liver and the really gross crap first so that you can get it out of the way while you're already feeling awful and things like flavor don't really matter.

Even before these ribs and their little green things, when it seemed like there was plenty of Dad left, Mom was getting it wrong. In fact, right off the bat, things were bad. On the third night of our grieving, and the first night of our dining, we were sitting at the table and not saying a word. In a way, that was appropriate (Dad loved steaks, and he liked quiet things, like fishing). And I guess it was interesting to get a direct taste of Dad like that right away, but it felt like too much, too soon.

I mean, I know that everyone does it, but it's weird to see meat on your plate and know that it came from the guy you read a book with the week before. I liked the Potter series, but it was kind of sad, reading some dumb book so that we could pretend like Dad wasn't dying. I would've said, "Fuck it," if I'd had any better suggestion, but I didn't really. And Mom would've yelled at me for cursing. But maybe Dad wouldn't have told her. It was just him and me, because Mom and Dad decided that even Harry Potter is a little too scary for my sister after the Dementors appeared in the third book.

I guess that it was nice to have the alone time with my dad, too, even if it was just reading about magical people in a made-up part of a real country. Dad was half in and half out, and I read out loud and pretended that I could remember anything I was reading. But I must have held onto some of it. When I sat down to my steak, I did think about my mom and house elves and how fucked up things are, even if I can't say "fucked up" at the dinner table. I'd like to tell Mom that her ribs are fucked up tonight, but it's not really the ribs that are fucked up. It's that we have all of these parts of the grieving process that we're supposed to do, and they're supposed to make us feel better, but now that we're at the end of it, I hate the ribs, and I hate the world for letting my dad die, and I even hate my dad a little for dying. Now that's fucked up.

On steak night, I wasn't the first to take a bite of the actual meat. That was my sister. She had Mom cut it for her. I think Mom and I both watched Ashleigh take her bite, but neither of us really faced her. Like it always is with little kids, it's pretty easy to know what Ashleigh is feeling. When Dad was dying, she cried all of the time. It was kind of nice, because it let me fade into the background, but it was kind of a pain, because it could be a pain in the ass, too. Like when a car alarm goes off and the owner doesn't silence it. On steak night, Ashleigh chewed it a little, and it looked like there was a moment where she was thinking about spitting it out, but she ended up swallowing it. Then she went on to the potatoes. Bad sign. Come to think of it, tonight, she's poked at the ribs without actually taking a bite yet. I suppose that the curiosity of how Dad tastes is long gone. Even more gone than Dad.

I'd never asked any of the kids at school what people taste like, but I'd overheard some of them talking about it. Danny Olsen's mom had a heart attack when we were in fifth grade, and for the next month, a lot of people would talk to him, trying to comfort him. But I think we all kind of knew the real reason why they were talking to him, too. There was something magical about him now. One day, while I was playing Blaster Man (I know, you never think about how stupid the hero names are when you're a kid) with a couple of the other boys, I was hiding by the trees on the parking lot side of the playground. Danny and some other kids were sitting by the trees, digging at the ground. "So, it's not like chicken?" one of the kids said.

Danny snorted. He kind of mumbled something that I couldn't catch, then he said, "Anyway, I can tell you've never tasted it." It was a harsh thing to say. How could the kid have known? It's not like it was her fault. But maybe Danny was just working through his grief or whatever the guidance counselors called it. I guess I haven't done all that much better. After calling the other kid out, Danny kind of looked around. It looked like he was acting, to be honest. Like he knew this was a big moment for him. Before this, I think the most attention Danny ever got was for doing well at the geography bee we had the previous year. Not exactly a shooting star. Though I actually let myself take some free cookies from Mrs. Schmidt at the bakery a couple days after Dad died, so I can't really judge.

So anyway, Danny looked around, shook his head, and said, "It tastes like death. That's what it tastes like." The other kids nodded, like they knew. One of them, I think it was Shelly Steinmetz, caught me looking, and I wandered off. I sort of felt bad, but not really. Shelly was always hanging around the cool kids, and Danny probably would've appreciated the attention of one more kid listening to him. If it makes it any better, I got killed by one of the other kids playing Blaster Man. He came running by, pointed his finger at my chest and yelled, "Zap.".] I said, "Whatever," and went to where the line would eventually leave from for all of us to go in after recess was over.

But here's the thing about hearing Danny Olsen talk, and I know this is stupid: I thought that my parents might have tasted differently than Danny's mom. I get that it's not like you can tell the difference between burgers if they come from different cows. In fact, probably each burger comes from a few different cows. I assume that a bunch of cows are chopped up and tossed in a big grinder or something, so every burger that you get is a mix of different cows, but probably the same herd. I'm not sure what I'm trying to say. But the point is that I walked away from Danny talking about how his mom tasted, and I thought that it would be different for me. I guess it's hard to say what exactly "death" would taste like, so it sort of was the same, but maybe not really. If death tastes like charcoal and how dog food smells and that feeling in the back of your throat before you start crying, then my dad did taste like death.

Anyway, the first night of eating Dad was bad, but it was bad in the way that things are always bad for "the grieving family." The next few nights were weirdly even. The shock started to wear off a little, but as that happened, the quality of what we were eating went down. I don't mean the quality of Dad. He had set things up with a butcher to make sure that his body was correctly preserved and cut up. It's more how we were served. From steak to these crappy tacos to liver. I mean, we knew that it had to come sometime, but I'd never even had liver before. The steak, I could know that it should taste better, under different circumstances. But liver sounded gross, looked gross, and smelled gross.

It made me think that the people whose parents died from a car accident were the luckiest ones. If someone's parents died because they were hit by not just a car, but a semi, then a lot of the meat would end up on the fenders, the road and wherever. I mean, I know that would be gross and traumatic or whatever, but at least it would be all over the place, and that would help "the grieving family" in two ways. First, it would mean that there would be less meat for you to have to work through. Let's be honest: Nobody would take the time to scrape every little bit of meat off the cars, so you have less to work through. Second, the parent meat would be like cows. It would be all the same pile: muscle, kidneys, liver, and so on. I guess that it's bad, because you might end up eating some of the things like eyes or toenails, but it's less bad, because it's all in one mix, so you don't have to end up eating the kidney and liver separately.

It's funny, because I remember asking my dad about different weird things that they ate in the Harry Potter books when the first couple came out, before Dad got sick. "Dad, what's 'treacle'?" "Dad, what's pumpkin juice?" And he always knew. For treacle, he even bought us some molasses cookies so that we could get an idea of what it would kind of taste like, though Ashleigh was too young to know why we were eating them. But it's still a nice memory. And if I get anything from eating Dad, I hope it's his goodness. Mom says that the belief that we get the strength or bravery or wisdom of the dead by eating them is superstition. Eating your family, according to Mom, is something that people "just do." But, if you can actually absorb something, then what I want to absorb is my dad's basic goodness. I want to be calm and kind and patient like my dad. Which I'm not right now. I'm usually horny and confused and kind of pissed off. It's hard not to be pissed off when you're horny and confused a lot, I think.

I'm sure that Dad would have wanted me to have some of his goodness, but he probably wouldn't call it goodness. He was a good guy, but he wouldn't have said that about himself. The problem is that if he tried to put a little of himself in me, then he'd be like Lord Voldemort, and his goodness would be a horcrux. I think. I guess it would depend on whether he was putting his goodness in me (and I know how that sounds) to make me good or to have people say that he raised a really nice kid. I don't think that people say that I'm a really nice kid. But I don't think that people say much about me at all. I know I'm not a football player or an honors student or someone who knows how to cook their father, but I'm also not a dick or a bully or a drunk. And that should count for something. But, I know, as I sit here and look down at the last of my father, if I really want to not be a dick, then I need to eat it and not hurt Mom's feelings. It's what my dad would want and it's what my dad would do, and it might be the best shot I have at getting some of his goodness in me. And I guess that says something about goodness; that it's more like something you have to keep doing, and you have to keep doing for other people, like when Harry...well, I guess I shouldn't drop a spoiler.

But it's not a spoiler to say that I want to be like Harry Potter, and not in the way that he's special or that he's magical. I mean that I'll be like him because I'm going to do the shit that I need to do. I'm sure that seems lame when what you have to do is just eat your dad's ribs, but my dad's life was a lot of crap, especially towards the end. And so that's what I do. I pick up a rib and I eat and I smile. Even though it wasn't that good.

Susan Knecht

The Hijab

At the clothing store, Nisreen was grateful for the yards of cotton covering her arms and legs and the niqab that hid her face but allowed for a strip around the eyes so she could see. She last wore the hijab in Syria, the hem of the black flowing garment a shade lighter on the petrol-soaked desert roads, and when they first moved to Toledo, but not since. After marrying Johnny she no longer felt the need.

"How much is this one?" Nisreen held up the black gabardine suit in a youth size small.

"That one? Let me see." The clerk, a middle-aged man with a potbelly straining the buttoned-down vest of his three-piece suit, ran his finger down the price list.

They would be lucky if anything fit: Amir was well fed but clothes always seemed to hang on him like drapery. Her mother said Nisreen was much the same at that age, but after Amir's birth, her body became fuller and she watched every little thing she ate. Nisreen's family came over years before the latest trouble with Assad. Her father, a physics professor with a solid reputation in Syria, settled with Nisreen and her mother into the mid-Western university life of a tenure-tracked academic. The moment Nisreen saw all the smart young women on campus, she begged her father to enroll her too. After all, in Damascus her grades were top of the class, enough to merit a scholarship. Grudgingly, her father consented.

"That's two hundred even. Plus tax." The rosacea on the clerk's cheeks and nose gave him a harried, nervous look.

If Johnny had bothered coming he would have thrown her an anxious glance. But he had bills to sort through and a migraine besides, he said. His adjunct lecturer position at the local university ran out of funding in the spring and, without it, their health insurance would soon be just another luxury. Her purse vibrated against her hip. Inside the main compartment next to her wallet, a photograph of Johnny and his half cocky grin, half smile lit up her iPhone. It was taken last July at the Apple store; Johnny was rather proud of himself for buying her a new model after the last one stopped working.

"Any luck?" Johnny sounded farther away than the three short miles their house was from the mall, but in the last few years of their marriage he had sounded even farther away than that only sitting a few feet from her in the living room.

"I'm still looking," Nisreen said with irritation. He had already called twice on the drive over but she ignored him both times. How like him to choose the exact moment she was thinking of him. He was like a hound that could sniff out any little attention thrown his way.

"Remember: nothing too expensive. The funeral alone is costing us a fortune."

"But I told you my mom and dad would help with that," she whispered closely into the phone while the clerk pretended to straighten the shelves.

"I don't know why you think he needs a proper suit anyway," Johnny huffed. "He only ever wore jeans and a T-shirt."

"Because it's important to me."

In the background came the somber melodramatic narration from another of those "True Crime" stories he was so fond of watching.

Much to her poor parents' chagrin, Nisreen had already consented to forego the traditional Islamic service; allowing their son to be buried in a suit was Johnny's one concession, and even that was a fight. But Nisreen could not envision her son's death without a proper suit. Otherwise she would wait every day by the bay windows for the squeaky sound of his bicycle wheels on the pavement and continue to change the sheets on his bed. No. Death could not come without the costume. "Aren't you too busy for this?" She sniffs into the phone. "I thought you had bills to pay."

"What? I do. I'm taking a break. Just don't spend too much time there—"

Nisreen shoved the phone back in her purse. "Have you got anything less expensive?" Her voice caught. She could visit another store but the funeral was tomorrow, and they desperately needed the suit today. Her son's only other option, the little corduroy jacket with tiny patches on the elbows, still hung in his closet at home. The last time Amir wore it he was four years old and riding a scooter at their family friend's wedding. The niqab muffled her sob. Even if Johnny wouldn't forgive her for spending the money, a wiry boy of sixteen should not be laid out in an open coffin wearing a brown corduroy suit four sizes too small.

"Let me check the inventory." The clerk produced a binder from beneath the register.

Nisreen met Johnny the first day of the fall semester. No other boy would have dared speak to her in the hijab but something about Johnny was different. A lecturer in Biology, he wore a tracksuit most days although he later admitted he wasn't a runner. He simply didn't feel comfortable in zippers and seams. After hardly exchanging a few words all semester, she was more than a little surprised when he returned her final paper with his phone number written at the top in red ink. Such a thing could have risked his job—at the time, sexual harassment claims were rampant on campus, although Nisreen would never have reported him. For what, a friendly gesture? Later on when they started seeing each other, he apologized for being too forward. His family was Mormon, and he hadn't dated much.

"You don't even know what I look like," she said with complete surprise when he stopped her outside of class the day after he returned her paper.

"I know enough," Johnny said. She liked how, when she looked at him, he held her gaze for a second or two longer than most people she had met.

"Is it for a particular occasion?" The clerk blinked expectantly.

Nisreen bristled. Americans. Always with their invasive questions.

From the very first day in her new country, the pinched white faces on the bank line and the false gaiety from the cashier at the taco drive-in were enough to make Nisreen scream. "Can I take your order?" the girl in the baseball cap trilled every time Johnny pulled the lemon-yellow Hyundai up to the drive-through window. It was as though somehow American society expected her to forget that the insurgents detonated their city into oblivion, and that her family had barely escaped Damascus with their lives.

They should never have moved to this backwater town. Nisreen only ever agreed to it to please Johnny—because a wife must defer to her husband's wishes, her father said, and you'll only be a short plane ride away. Her mother had always deferred in their marriage and her mother before her, but many a late evening Nisreen saw her mom crying into the pot of boiling Mulukhiyah on the stove when her dad still hadn't returned home after work.

"Ma'am?" The clerk offered another gratuitous American smile, all white dentures and too much gum.

"It's for my son's funeral."

"Oh. I see." The clerk cleared his throat and closed the binder. "My condolences for your loss," he said with an easy compassion. Emerging from behind the counter, he was shorter than he appeared at the cash register. "Let me show you what we have on sale."

She steadied herself against the glass counter; the hijab would make her stronger. She would hide in its shadows as she had always done, concealing happiness or pain or fear. After years of the hijab hanging in mothballs in the hall closet, she had walked into the living room that morning covered from head to toe in black.

"I don't recognize you," Johnny said, looking up from his book.

"I was wearing it when you first met me."

When they first started dating, it was Nisreen's decision to stop wearing it. Her parents never recovered.

"We should never have allowed her to study at university," her father said.

"We should have never left my family in Syria," her mother said.

"But you haven't worn it in years. What's changed?" Johnny's reading glasses slid down his short nose.

"Our son is dead."

He adjusted his glasses and returned to his book.

Amir's arrival changed things for the better. A happy soul, he delighted in the smallest things. The baby's sparkling chestnut eyes followed every motion of his father's pen as Johnny graded freshman papers. He was an early walker and a late talker; Nisreen's parents doted on the boy with lavish gifts on his birthday and the promise of his own car when he turned seventeen. In time, after several circular arguments, they quit insisting she bring him to the mosque for Qur'an study.

When Amir grew a wispy beard in high school and asked a litany of questions about Islam, Nisreen said it was his choice whether or not he wanted to be observant. Frowning in his armchair, Johnny adamantly insisted they were atheists. "Speak for yourself," she fired back. At night before bed and before any big decision, Nisreen still whispered full-hearted prayers to Allah. She might have given up her hijab but never her God.

When he was three years old, Amir learned the bedtime prayer; they recited it together in Arabic, the blue light of the Captain America nightlight illuminating the boy's round face. She couldn't have known he would repeat the Arabic words out loud at school his senior year. But Amir insisted: If they make us say the Pledge of Allegiance during assembly, then he could recite the prayer. Once when she picked him up from track practice, he pointed someone out to Nisreen, a strange boy who sat in the last row and was left back twice. He plays video games on his smartphone for target practice, Amir said. Nisreen couldn't help noticing he was a good head taller than most of the other students.

The day before he died, Amir came home bleeding from the head and mouth.

"Call 911," Johnny said, frantically patting the pockets of his jacket for his mobile.

"He needs a new school," Nisreen said, dialing the number with trembling fingers. But they couldn't afford private.

The paramedics cleaned up their son. The next day, after making her way past the glum security guard and through the school's metal detector, Nisreen sat across a crowded desk from Mr. Phillips, the school principal, an avuncular type with pockmarked skin. She wore a smart skirt suit with sheer stockings but her legs felt bare, and her angular face and blue-black hair were cruelly exposed.

"I would take him back to Syria but we'd never get back into the U.S.," she told Mr. Phillips tearfully. The authorities were afraid of terrorists, and too many of their family friends had been denied reentry after the travel ban. But there was no travel ban on the left-back kid who kept a gun in his locker.

Mr. Phillips smiled sympathetically, but offered no solution. Nisreen ground her teeth painfully at the irony: to escape the frying pan only to burn in the fire. She shouldn't have left Damascus; she should be shivering with the others behind hollowed-out supermarket walls, covering her ears at the shattering bursts of IEDs in the distance. If her son had never been born he would have been spared the insult of the left-back boy's rough hands around his skinny neck and, too late, the violent crack of the wadcutter bullet that shattered his spine. At the morgue when the coroner lifted the sheet, Johnny covered his mouth in horror at the dark unfathomable hole in Amir's chest as Nisreen tore out handfuls of her own hair in anguish.

For Johnny, what happened was an anomaly, some random bad luck, but for Nisreen, it was written from the very beginning.

"So many guns in this country," she had said on their first date for frozen yogurt at the mini-mall. On the second floor next to the arcade, the gun store ran a brisk business. It's the price you pay for freedom, Johnny said, offering her some of his strawberry cheesecake flavor. Pluralism, he said, was a complicated thing, hard to pin down, like a moving target. "Then how did you catch me?" Nisreen smiled and Johnny did too, his dimples surfacing briefly.

Like most big questions, it was left unresolved. From time to time, however, they did revisit the issue. Once while washing dishes, she noted that Amir's high school looked more like a prison than a place of learning, and Johnny asked, "Would you rather he be killed by a terrorist's mortar in Syria?"

"I would rather he not be killed by anything at all, thank you very much," Nisreen said, drying the last china plate.

As the clerk fussed with the rack of suits, Nisreen hid her hands in the pockets of her hijab shamefully: She had removed the gold wedding band that morning and her fingernails were bitten to the nub.

"Is this a better choice?" The clerk held up a simple black suit that looked to be the right size. "It's half off."

"Yes. That's more like it." They could afford one hundred dollars if they paid the utilities late and canceled the cable. She would call Johnny and tell him.

The clerk removed the hanger and laid out the suit carefully on the glass counter like a cadaver. "Will this be cash or charge?"

Nisreen searched her purse for the wallet and frowned: there were no bills in the billfold. "Do you accept personal checks?" She asked tentatively, like a teenager hoping to borrow the car.

"I'm sorry ma'am, but we don't."

Nisreen closed her eyes. Without the suit there could be no funeral. Without the funeral there could be no death. Without the death there could be no Amir, and before the baby was ever conceived, there could have been other choices. Nisreen shivered. She wished she never married Johnny. They were clearly unsuited for one another. Like her father, consolation, or anything emotional for that matter, was beyond him, and he preferred the microscope and a dry equation to a heart to heart. For more than a year they had tried for a baby, and on the occasion of their second anniversary, when she told Johnny she was pregnant, he teared up. But when they embraced, his jacket smelled of perfume. They never said spoke about it after that. Not until their son was born did they start talking in earnest again, and always about the baby. Now that Amir was gone, they would have nothing to say to one another anymore.

At her gloomy silence, the clerk reconsidered. "Alright, a personal check will be fine. I'll need to see some identification."

Nisreen nodded appreciatively. Americans, when they weren't shooting each other and hating people different from themselves, could be generous too. She made out the check to "Ehrlich's Suits and Accessories," and endorsed it with the practiced flourishes she first learned in grade school in Damascus. The clerk glanced at the photo on Nisreen's driver's license and then at her niqab, and when she removed the covering for a moment, like most American men, he reddened at a glimpse of her unadorned face. Feeling naked, she quickly pulled the niqab back in place.

Thanks to American justice, in the few days since the shooting Amir's murderer was already out on bail. She never told Johnny but she had considered ringing the doorbell of the boy who killed her only son and strangling him where he stood. A swift retribution would save them all the trouble of a trial. With her hands squeezing hard around his throat, the pasty boy would stand there making choking sounds, the dyed-black locks of hair falling over his bulging eyes, and afterwards her parents would visit her in prison. She would wear an orange suit and avoid their fearful questions. She could never bear her mother's tears or her father's regret.

After tomorrow, once Amir is lowered into the ground and the mourners have all left, she thinks she will go home and, still wearing the hijab, climb into the bathtub with Johnny's new razorblade from Walmart. He will find another wife, another job, another home. Besides the hijab, Nisreen will never find anything again she might call her own.

"My condolences again." The clerk handed her the shopping bag with the suit wrapped in tissue paper inside.

Marie C. Lecrivain

What They Need to Hear

I.

Apollo finds a long line of the faithful coiled around his temple spiraling outward into the dusty foothills. He smiles. *Yes. Business is booming,* he tells himself, *but the franchises need equal distribution. The shareholders are definitely not happy.*

He considers his next move. Apollo knows his horny father's left a trail of hoofprints and feathered destruction between here and Cyprus. He decides to become one of the *little* people. Apollo bows his shoulders like Atlas, drinks a cup of black coffee to stain the white of his smile, unlaces his sandals, and stashes his lyre into a battered guitar case. He rubs earth into his hair, and behold; he's now a 99%er, albeit a little too good-looking, but the day is hot, and the line is long, so perhaps no one will notice.

II.

Apollo, aka Mr. Hipster, takes his place at the end of the line. He wonders what's become of the world he once knew, the one he once looked down upon in his daily sunrise travels while cruising in his celestial Porsche with one million kelvin horsepower and rhino leather interior. The former green-and-blue world is now stained brown and gray.

He wonders when the sacrifices, libations, and jingles the bards wrote in his honor will resume.

Where have all the tributes gone?

He's never asked his worshipers for much: a few nymphs to seduce, a crown of sonnets, a handful of coins—every day—this is what he requires. He's nothing like his twin sister, Artemis, who demands all aspirants become lifetime members of PETA and invest all their savings into the growth of turbine wind-power farms. Nor is he like his brother, Ares, who spends his devotees' donations on manufacturing cheap chariots and subpar body armor, and then sells them back to his favorite warmongers at 3,000% profit.

No. Apollo doesn't understand their ways or their reasoning.

Where did we go wrong? Apollo asks himself.

Perhaps the answer is among mortals. He fine-tunes his heavenly ears to listen to the whispers within the hearts of men.

The wailing of ten thousand whiners crashes against the surface of Apollo's mind. He tries not to flinch at the tsunami of misery. Apollo knows the key to successful customer retention is active listening, so he lets the tides of complaint wash over him. The lightest float to the top:

I can't conceive a child.

I need a good 401K plan.

I want to buy a hut, but I have shitty credit.

These are everyday concerns, not ones Apollo allows his oracles to spend more than five minutes ruminating. They're not worth chewing laurel leaves.

He dives in deeper, searches for true misery and finds more of the same.

I work two jobs, and I still can't pay my rent.

My wife has cancer and our insurance stopped covering her chemo treatments.

I've been unemployed for three years. No one will hire me.

I'm a veteran of the Peloponnesian Wars, and the government cut my benefits.

Apollo becomes frustrated, as these are—again—everyday concerns. Why are there so *many* people *here,* instead of at one of the other three friendly locations? He just installed a new coffee bar at Delphi. For an extra 50 drachmas, aspirants can now receive expedited prophecies.

Apollo realizes the answers can't be found in the hearts of men, so he turns off his heavenly hearing, cracks his neck, and sighs.

III.

Behind Apollo, the line has stretched beyond the farthest point a mortal man can see. Astounded, Apollo finds himself at the bottom of the temple steps and wonders how much time has passed. Tapping on the pilgrim's shoulder in front of him, he asks, *Dude, what time is it? I left my portable sundial at home.*

The pilgrim shrugs. *It's mid-morning, but hopefully, I'll be able to meet with the oracle. They close for lunch at 11:30... I've been in line for two days.*

Apollo considers this information carefully. With trepidation, he asks, *There's other oracles you could visit. Why are you waiting so long for* this *one?*

The pilgrim smiles and utters one word. *Orpheus.*

IV.

Apollo waits patiently waits as the line moves forward. He watches the pilgrims, one after the other, enter the shrine, a modest arch lit by the light of lavender-and-thyme-scented candles. He watches each pilgrim emerge with a satisfied smile on their face and realizes this is what he's *not* seen in a very long time: the *Sign of Satisfaction,* the guarantee of customer loyalty.

V.

It's Apollo's turn to enter the shrine. He looks around for a temple maiden to take his payment—and finds none.

He walks slowly through the arch. Inside, he finds none of the usual trappings. *Gone* is the 50-foot gold statue of Apollo's radiant being. *Erased* are the frescoes of his sexual exploits. *Vanished* is the marble prie-dieu for the pilgrims to kneel upon. In its place is a simple three-legged stool placed near a wooden pedestal upon which sits the head of Orpheus, eyes closed, a faint frown on his pale face.

Apollo regards the silent face of Orpheus, and wonders, *How long can an immortal go without sleep... and without dreams?*

Apollo seats himself on the stool, stretches out his legs, opens his guitar case, and pulls out his lyre. Setting his hands to the strings, he plays a soft melody meant for Orpheus' ears alone. He watches the face of Orpheus gradually change; the frown bend upwards into a smile and the lines recede from his brow.

Once he's through, Apollo puts away his lyre. Orpheus's eyes open; one green, the other black, long-ago reminders of his adventures upon the earth, and below.

I miss music, says Orpheus. A single tear drips down his face. *I miss the feel of the lyre in my hands.*

Apollo stares into the eyes of Orpheus.

My son, you're taking business away from the other temples, Apollo says. *Why?*

Orpheus says nothing.

Apollo cracks his knuckles, a staccato chorus that reverberates through the shrine.

Orpheus, he says, *I have to know what you're doing differently, and why.*

Orpheus sighs, a long melodic breath that sends a shiver up Apollo's spine.

It's not what I've done, he says, his eyes filled with tears. *It's what's been done to me, left to rot forever in this room, an eternal sympathetic ear for the world's problems. I never asked for this. I never asked for this... but what's there to do, other than listen and give them the one answer that fits every inquiry.*

What answer? Apollo asks.

There are worse things than suffering, answers Orpheus, *all of this will pass away. They'll never truly die...*

VI.

The melodic symphony in Orpheus' tears can only be heard by Apollo, who then reaches out and caresses the back of his son's head.

Orpheus, my boy, Apollo says. *I'm sorry, but you're fired.*

I figured as much, Orpheus says, *but what shall become of me? May I die now?*

Gently, Apollo picks up the head of Orpheus, opens his guitar case, and tucks it in beside the lyre. *We'll discuss that as soon as I come up with an answer to satisfy the shareholders.*

Marlene Olin

Becca and Jamie

Becca comes home grinning from her first real job. Suspicious stains blotch her T-shirt. Dog hair velcros her jeans. But she is happy. Running into the kitchen, she grabs the calculator on her mother's desk and totals the day's earnings. Then she finds a pad and sits down at the table. For the next twenty minutes, she compiles a list of everything forty-nine dollars can buy.

Dog food!!! $25.00
A New E-book!!! $10.00
Socks!!! $10.00
Frozen Pinkberry Yogurt!!! $4.00

Her mother Alma doesn't have the heart to tell her about Social Security, Medicare, and withholding tax. She puts that task on a shelf and mentally assigns it to her husband. Rick is an accountant and the yang to Alma's yin. Left-brained. Linear and logical. For now, she lets her daughter bask in the glow of her good fortune. Becca is eighteen years old. Though she needs her parents' help, there is nothing she craves more than independence.

"How did it go?" Alma's at the sink washing dishes, her back turned, prying but not prying.

"We had five poodles, three Bichons, a Maltese, a King Charles, a Havanese, and a German Shepherd. The Shepherd had a bad case of mange. It was truly disgusting."

"And?" asks Alma. There's always more, some pertinent information casually overlooked.

"Fernando lent me his tweezers. I plucked three ticks out of the Bichon, two out of a poodle, and one out of my upper triceps." Rolling up her sleeve, Becca runs her finger over an invisible spot. Back and forth. Back and forth.

The two have their own Morse code. A word here. A word there. A long pause. Alma watches her daughter's reflection in the toaster. Becca is humming and smiling, the muscles unstrained, her face a soft, kneaded lump.

The following Saturday the same ritual plays out. Alma picks Becca up at the pet groomer's. Her daughter formulates a new spending list. Then they stretch out the entire week, buying every item on the list one day at a time. Their days are filled with errands—the food store, the dry cleaners, the bank—interspersed with stabs at programmed exercise.

Alma glances at her calendar. This week they are trying aerobics on Monday, tai chi on Tuesday, spin cycling on Wednesday, belly dancing on Thursday, karate on

Friday. They show up to each class in identical outfits and shiny sneakers. As usual, they linger long after the rest of the class has left.

"Becca, you've got to look in the mirror," the aerobics instructor says. "Bend your knees. Roll your shoulders." But the image in the mirror is a stranger, a person whose arms and legs go in random directions. No matter how hard Becca concentrates, she can't will her body to be graceful. She's like a stick figure come to life, a jumble of arms and legs with minds of their own.

"Maybe she should try Pilates," suggests the instructor. "Or yoga."

Alma wipes the sweat off her forehead with her wristband. Whatever hoops she makes her daughter jump through, she forces herself to undertake as well. She forgets the instructor's name—it's something edible like Brie or Brandy. She looks in her thirties, old enough to be a mother, old enough to have sampled a dollop of pain.

Alma edges close enough to see the perspiration bubbling on the woman's chest. The bubbles sit there, plump.

"My daughter loves music," she whispers. "We've tried dance classes but she can't keep up." Desperate, Alma begs. "Maybe she can stand right behind you. Maybe if she were close enough, she could follow your steps."

Alma has long ago learned to swallow her pride. There is no level to which she will not stoop. She is her daughter's advocate in all things. Becca has walked over to a window. The throbbing drumbeat of the music is still playing in her head. She shifts from one foot to the other, her happy stance, humming and tapping the glass.

Alma figures she has around ten percent of the instructor's attention. She watches her bend over, pack her stretch bands and CD player in a tote, tighten the ponytail on her head. As she leaves the gym, the instructor finally glances over her shoulder and appraises Alma from the bottom up. The words spurt out like gunfire. "Dance is fast. Aerobics is fast." Opening the door, she plants one leg in the hall. "Life is fast."

In a year's time, Becca will be starting college at the state university three hours away. A cabal of professionals suggested that she take a year off. A growth year, they called it. A year to mature. Her husband Rick says not to worry. Since when does Alma worry?

Becca, of course, has her bags packed. All of the kids she went to high school with have started new lives and new adventures. But she has no idea what pitfalls await her, what booby traps are ready to be sprung. Alma sees them in 3-D with Dolby sound. They are like the obstacles of a video game. Barrel your way through class registration. Hurdle insensitive professors. Bypass sororities and fraternities in turbo drive.

The coursework is manageable, say the professionals. Tutors can be hired. There are people who help organizationally challenged students organize their time. But what keeps Alma up at night are the known unknowns. Who will invite Becca to a football game or a movie? Who will sit next to her in the cafeteria when she has her meals? Of all the challenges they both have faced, this is the hardest problem to fix.

Without her mother by her side, Becca is alone. When she was younger, other disabled children kept her company. But as Becca progressed, as the charts and graphs showed her inching closer to normal, her social skills lagged behind.

Becca is stuck in a twilight zone, a murky limbo of lost souls. As she exits her teenage years, she is too high functioning to live among low-functioning adults and too quirky to be accepted by anyone else. She is and is not a success story. Meanwhile, Alma fills the gaps. They are constant companions. Each month they bleed in sync.

The following Saturday Becca comes home with one side of her face sunburn red. Her clothes look windblown, like she walked through a hurricane.

"It's really hot under the dryer, Mom."

She opens the door of the refrigerator and drinks a quart of orange juice straight from the container. Then she stands there with the door open, waiting for the cold air to lower her body temperature. Alma pries without prying. Finally, the words spill out.

"They won't let me do anything but dry the dogs. The dryer is huge and hot and sometimes I get dizzy it's so hot. Jamie washes and I dry."

"Can't you switch?" asks Alma. "Can't you wash for a while?"

The memory of it makes Becca crumble. In seconds, she's sitting on the floor with her arms wrapped tightly around her waist. Her head's down. She's talking to the ground, her body rocking like it's at sea.

"I had trouble with the hose. I kinda got Jamie wet, Fernando wet, the walls wet."

Fernando, the owner, has groomed the family dogs for years. Alma doubted he would trust Becca with clippers or scissors but bathing the dogs seemed probable. Plausible. A way Becca could be helpful—but then again maybe not.

Alma pictures the calendar pages flipping. In twelve months' time she is pushing this child out the door. It takes every ounce of energy to resist stomping into the groomer's and chewing Fernando's ear. The hardest thing Alma does is to do absolutely nothing at all.

•••

Becca slowly learns. The next week, she stands a foot further away and repositions the blower. The heat is still intense but bearable. Her cohort in crime, the washer named Jamie, invites her to walk to a convenience store to have an Icee during their break. For years Becca has been kept on a rigid diet. No gluten, no milk, no artificial additives, no refined sugars. She gulps a dozen different vitamins a day.

But the five-minute walk to the convenience store is an unexpected treat. She is purchasing something with her own money. She has made a friend. And she is wise enough and smart enough to realize how special the moment is.

For the first time in her life, Becca slurps frozen Coca-Cola. Even though a yard-long list of admonitions plays in her mind, she pretends to like it. Of course, she would have preferred a carrot/green bean/kale shake from Whole Foods. But Whole Foods isn't walking distance from Canine Couture. And her new friend Jamie hates healthy food. Just hates it!

Becca imagines a radio and turns the knob. She is adjusting to Jamie's bandwidth. She is trying to be flexible. She pictures a rubber band that can stretch and stretch and stretch.

"It's like so easy to get a fake ID," Jamie tells Becca.

Her new friend likes to talk. Jamie has worked for Fernando for almost a year, dumping flea-bitten mongrels into vats of insecticide, combing out turds that seem glued on. Jamie's twenty-one and goes clubbing at every opportunity.

"We could hang out," says Jamie. "It'll be fun."

Becca feels her eyes growing larger by the second.

"Give me your number." Jamie pulls out a cell phone. "What night is good for you?" A poised index finger is ready to punch. "Of course, we'll have to clean you up. Do your hair. Put on some makeup."

•••

Each night, Becca locks herself in her bedroom for hours. The computer has always been her confidante, her guru, her guide. It is the world contained within a box, rule-driven and manageable. Meanwhile, Alma stands outside her door. She is listening yet not listening, knowing that the computer robs her daughter like a thief. There's no telling what sort of trouble a kid like Becca could get into on the internet. Her whole life could become the internet. While Becca is in the shower, Alma races to her desk and checks her search history.

Usually, Becca watches cute pet videos on YouTube. She'll follow link after link of *health alerts!!!* then empty the pantry of plastic containers and the bathroom cabinets of suspect soaps. But last month she asked for a new set of headphones. This month a huge MasterCard bill arrived in the mail. Becca's been scrolling iTunes, spending obscene quantities of money listening to the latest pop hits.

At dinner, she leaves her parents speechless.

"Jamie is picking me up at tomorrow at eight. We're going clubbing."

A bowl of quinoa sits next to a plate of stir-fried tofu. Alma puts her fork down on her plate. She swallows slowly. Becca is too honest to ever lie to her parents. They are so lucky lucky lucky that she never lies. Becca trusts them with the blind obedience of a dog. Alma searches the room for the dog. She wants to kick the dog.

Rick speaks first. "Jamie is the girl you work with, right? The washer, right?"

Becca stares at the ceiling. "I'm not sure."

Alma wills her heart to keep on pumping, concentrates on big fat globules of blood making their way through her too skinny arteries. "What do you mean, Sweetie?"

"I mean," says Becca, "that it's confusing."

She heads towards her bedroom and retrieves a pencil sketch. Becca's desk is filled with drawings of dogs and cats. She rarely tackles people, their ever-changing features a mystery beyond her grasp. She lays the paper on the kitchen table. "See? She's kinda like a mutt. She's a little bit of everything."

Staring at them is the strangest-looking person Alma has ever seen. The hair is like a woman's. Long, flowing to the shoulders. The mouth is pursed in a coy smile. But the jaw is huge, the neck thick, the shoulders wide. Becca ran the side of her pencil over the cheekbones to darken the skin.

"Is Jamie black?" asks Alma. "Or maybe tanned?"

"When she doesn't shave," says Becca, "she has a beard."

Alma is counting in her head. She's up to seventeen and figures by the time she reaches fifty she'll be able to speak. Slowly her pulse throbs in time to the numbers. Eighteen. Nineteen. Twenty.

"I thought you had to be twenty-one," says Alma. "They serve alcohol in most of those clubs."

Becca stares at her mother's chin. Eye contact has always been difficult. Instead, she talks to your chin, your nose, a speck of lint on your shoulder. "Jamie knows the owner. It's a karaoke club. People dress in costumes and sing."

Finally, Rick speaks. "What's the worst that can happen?" he says.

A surge of hate swells in Alma's throat. Being the nice guy is easy. Parenting is hard. In seconds her brain formulates every possible roadblock, every argument she can throw at her daughter to convince her not to go, to demand that she not go.

Then she fast forwards a year's time. Soon Becca will be on her own. No one will be there to pick and choose her friends, to make these decisions. The plan is for Jamie to pick Becca up. At least, Alma figures, she'll be able to look over Jamie's car and while she's at it, look over Jamie.

But the plans don't go according to plan. Jamie lives an hour north in Hollywood. Not Hollywood, California, where the movie stars hang out, but Hollywood, Florida. On Saturday, an hour before the shop closes, Becca calls her mother. They're leaving directly from work, then driving to Jamie's house. The club is in Fort Lauderdale, another five miles north.

Her jeans are still clean, Becca assures her. Yes, she has money. Yes, she will be home by midnight. Yes, she will call at least once from the club.

Rick is sitting on the family room sofa, watching football on TV, eating his way through a bag of Doritos.

"All Becca needs to find are a bunch of cool kids. Smart kids." There are chips on his lap, the couch cushions, the floor. "The kind who pride themselves on being nerds."

Alma glances at a snow globe on the coffee table. They bought it for Becca on their last vacation alone together. When was it? Five, seven years ago? She imagined it would make a sizeable dent if she threw it at her husband's head.

"Real life is not *The Big Bang Theory*, Rick. Not everyone who is different has a genius I.Q. or twee clothes or a suitcase full of snappy retorts." She pours herself a glass of Merlot, but her hand is shaking so badly that half the blood-colored liquid splashes on the floor. "There's no laugh track in your daughter's life, Rick. There's no time-out for commercial breaks. Becca's walking a tightrope without a net and all we can do is look up and watch." Then she pops a Xanax for good measure and lies down on her bed.

•••

Hollywood is different. A Hard Rock Casino towers over blocks and blocks of concrete houses. Neon signs in strip malls wink and blink. Weeds thrive in the oddest of places. Sidewalk cracks. Rooftops. A small tree grows out of the asphalt in the middle of the street. Finally, the car stops.

Instead of grass, Jamie's front yard is mostly dirt. Someone has taken pieces of truck tires and lined the path to the front door. It looks like a black sea serpent is undulating up down up down trying to get inside.

"Me and my brother Sal live here," says Jamie.

Though Sal isn't home, his room is a living presence. Pizza boxes are stacked on the floor. Dirty socks and underwear are piled on the bed. It smells like B.O. and old soup. "My brother is a pig," says Jamie.

But Jamie's room is spotless. A teddy bear sits on the bed. Books about animals line the shelves.

Becca runs her fingers over the spines. "I didn't know you liked James Herriott!"

"There's a lot of things you don't know," Jamie answers. The world's largest makeup kit sits on a dresser. As if she's still at work, Jamie commands Becca to sit.

"In case you haven't figured it out, I'm halfway there," says Jamie. "If I ever have the money, I'll have an operation." To get her attention, her friend grabs Becca's chin. It is a gesture her mother has used thousands of times.

"Look at me, Becca. This is important. On the outside I'm a guy. I have a penis and carpet of hair I shave off my chest every day."

Becca tries hard not to blink. Blinking would be rude. Blinking and adequate eye contact do not peacefully coexist. But when she looks closely at Jamie's face, pores the size of manholes suddenly appear.

"But on the inside I'm a girl."

Once Becca starts blinking, it's hard to stop.

"Sure, I know I'm not pretty." On her nightstand are stacks of magazines. Jamie points to a celebrity on a cover. "But being pretty requires plastics I can't afford. So I'm neither here nor there. Stuck. In some sort of waiting room forever."

Jamie spends ten minutes applying lipstick and mascara to Becca's face and fixing her hair. Then she spends another half hour on her own, squeezes into a tight spandex dress, forces her large feet into a pair of heels. "How do I look?" she asks. Her voice is suddenly high and perky, as if someone took a magic wand and raised it an octave or two.

Becca glances at the magazines. All the people seem the same. Their lips pucker like fish. Their noses are nonexistent. Their eyes are scared and bulging. They look like they've seen a vampire or a werewolf or maybe even a ghost. Yes, that's it. A cartoon ghost. All at once, images of Scooby Doo and Shaggy flash before her. The clever TV tune pops into her head. For a brief moment, Becca shifts her feet, tilts her head, and hums.

Then she remembers where she is and who she's with and quickly reboots. Jamie is watching her, waiting for an answer. For the first time in her life, Becca lies. "You look great," she says. "Really beautiful. Just great."

She pats her friend's hand. It is another one of her mother's gestures. Becca resists the urge to count the black hairs curling on Jamie's wrist.

• • •

A month later, Alma finally gets to meet Jamie. A car with an indescribable paint color pulls up to their driveway. A tall person with a day-old beard in leggings and a sequined T-shirt knocks at their door. Becca makes the proper introductions. To Alma's shock, Jamie is the spitting image of her daughter's sketch.

"We're going clothes shopping, Mom. Jamie says it's never too soon to get ready for college."

Alma holds out her hand. *Take care of her* is on the tip of her tongue. But instead she says *Have fun.*

Elena Petrovic

Broken Doors and Happy Bears

Dad is going deaf.

He gets home from the doctor and shuts himself in his room. I follow, but Mom says to leave him alone, he doesn't want to talk right now. She tells me it is some rare viral infection in the left ear. I look at Dad's door and Bob Dylan stares back at me. Mom put up the poster last weekend, to hide the three dents. I made one of them, but it doesn't really count because I didn't mean to. I guess you could rationalize a lot of things that way.

Mom turns on the news, but she hardly watches. Her eyes are trained on the floor, her hands, anywhere but the screen. She notices me looking and offers a smile. She's very pretty, my mother. Tired-looking, but still pretty. After a while, she turns off the television and goes downstairs, probably to sleep in the guest room. The house is quiet and I slump down into the couch cushion. Light streams in from the living room window, highlighting every speck of dust and dog hair on the floor. I would clean them, but Dad smashed the vacuum last weekend. Mom said she could fix it, not to worry. I told her it was okay, I wasn't worried about a vacuum anyway.

The room is hot and empty, and it makes me feel sluggish. I am about to close my eyes when I hear the music. It drifts slowly from the hallway, and I lift my head to listen. It's Bob Dylan, but I don't know the song. Dad loves Bob Dylan. When I was little, he would play "Ring Them Bells" on the car stereo, over and over until the CD would start to skip. He would curse and blow on both sides of the disc, then try again. Sometimes it would work, the music would start, and he would slump back into his seat and smile. I remember watching him drive and thinking he looked beautiful. He had more hair then, but I thought so because his eyes got big and bright and soft. All at the same time. He wasn't a great singer, but it was nice how his voice rumbled along the track, slowly and a little off-key.

Dad is playing the song on full blast now. I get up and walk toward his room, my footsteps drowned in the blaring music. Bob Dylan guards the door, smoking his cigarette and looking down at me with cool blue eyes. I can't decide if he is good-looking or not, but I like his eyes. I apologize to them as I slowly tear down the poster. I can't have him protecting anyone right now. I step forward and run my fingers along the sloppily dented wooden holes. We just got new doors last spring.

I hear a clatter from within the bedroom and the music stops. Silence hangs heavy in the air. Silence, and then a sob. Shrill and child-like, it cuts through the wood and makes my stomach churn. My wrist turns the handle before I can stop myself and I see him curled in the covers, crying and shaking. I stand with my mouth slightly open. I should hold his hand or bring him water or call Mom, but I don't. I look at the door and I see him punch it, I hear him yell, I feel his rage. I inhale the same scent of his stale cigarettes and sadness.

Dad used to smell nice, like linen sheets and rain. He told me a story about rain once, when I was seven.

"Did you know that when the sun is shining and rain is falling, all of the bears in the world are getting married?"

I laughed out loud. It sounded silly, but I let him finish. He said that the bears made wedding veils out of flowers and rings out of tree bark. I smiled, and extended my little hand into the air. Suddenly the world seemed so fragile. The rain cascaded from the sky like glittering porcelain, and broke silently onto the ground. The flowers swayed and the air smelled of sweetness and perfumed petals. Everything was alive. I looked at Dad, and I knew he felt it too. We were similar. I pressed my head against his shoulder and I realized he had shown me beauty. He had a way of doing that, a long time ago. Now he just yells. Today, I guess, he cries.

"I can't hear it."

Dad is facing me. He wipes at his eyes and his face contorts into a pained smirk.

"I can't hear it," he repeats softly. His lips are quivering.

Dad grabs a book from the nightstand, slowly, and flings it at the wall. I might have flinched last year, but I don't even blink now. His chest heaves up and down. His breath comes out short and raspy, and he is shaking his head and whispering to himself. Fighting with himself, cursing at himself. He can't hear the music; the music that made him smile so sweetly and muse so quietly, years before the fighting and years before he started to look so old. I don't know what to say. I sit at the foot of his bed and look down at my hands. I see him from the corner of my eye and then he is hugging me, pressing into my shoulder and dripping reluctant tears down my shirt. I haven't hugged Dad in months, and his touch feels awkward and heavy. My skin goes hot and prickles in the places his tears drip down. I don't know if that is hatred, or even if I want it to be. I don't know where things fell apart and he stopped saying beautiful things. I don't know if any of that matters right now. I just hold him like he used to hold me, and I let him cry.

Steven B. Rosenfeld

Hickory Hill House

Felix Goldman sat alone in the high-beamed living room of Hickory Hill House on a Monday evening in mid-September, still struggling with Sunday's *New York Times* crossword puzzle. Felix had returned to the island inn for the third September since Anna's death, as they had done together for years, and the Sunday puzzle had always been part of it. But the puzzle was hardly a breeze for Felix without Anna to help him, particularly now that the editors had taken to including more current jargon and pop-culture references. Still, he carried the magazine section under his arm and kept a yellow pencil with a good eraser in his pocket, until he finished the puzzle in triumph (rarely) or abandoned it (usually).

Felix's concentration was interrupted this Monday evening by Charlie Young, the congenial proprietor of Hickory Hill House. Charlie rarely appeared in the living room after dinner, so Felix knew something was up.

"Felix!" Charlie said with evident pride. "I have a surprise for you—but it's a secret, so don't go telling the other guests. Anyway, now that I think about it, you're probably the only one here who would get excited about this."

What Charlie told him was this: later that week, he was expecting some very special guests, two names Felix instantly recognized, but, Charlie was right, none of the new crowd would know. They were both actors—they had appeared together on Broadway back in the '60s and '70s, and the husband had also been in many Hollywood films of that era. Felix remembered that he and Anna had seen them several times on the stage. He'd also been in some Hollywood films back then; hadn't he even been nominated once or twice for Best Supporting Actor? And would he ever forget her fiery red hair and her green eyes—not quite like Anna's, but close enough?

Charlie said they were coming to Hickory Hill House after dropping their granddaughter off at boarding school in Vermont because the wife would be appearing in an Off-Broadway play that was starting rehearsals soon, and she wanted a quiet place to learn her lines. Charlie assured him he could treat the newcomers as he would any other guests—please don't fawn over them, but it was fine to engage them in conversation and yes, as was the Hickory Hill custom, to call them Robert and Lynne.

"In fact, they said she'd be closeted in their room studying her script during the day," Charlie said, "so my guess is he'll be looking for company. I'd be grateful to you if you'd show him around a bit, Felix."

Felix could not suppress his excitement. No longer would he have to sit mute through dinner-table conversations about films he hadn't seen, books he hadn't read, and rock music, rather than the symphonies and opera he loved. With "Robert and Lynne" there would be lots to talk about. Even though Felix had cancelled the Philharmonic subscription after Anna's death and couldn't bring himself to go alone to every new play and opera production, as he and Anna had always done together, he was sure they could discuss theatre and music, old films, great books, perhaps the upcoming election. And Felix would be thrilled to show Robert around Hickory Hill.

•••

It would have been natural for the other guests at Hickory Hill House to question why a widower like Felix kept returning to the island alone every year. They might wonder why someone nearing 85, who no longer trusted himself behind the wheel, would endure the long bus ride to the ferry, and then wait for an island taxi to drive him up to Hickory Hill House. They could be forgiven some bewilderment about what drew him here alone, since his children and grandchildren lived far away and, for them, the island was just a distant memory.

None of them ever asked Felix why he still came. But if they had asked, he would say it was Hickory Hill itself, the elegant little inn on a rise in the center of the island, surrounded by 56 acres of pine, aspen, maple, oak, beech, and, of course, hickory, which now, in early September, was showing daily increasing bursts of bright yellow, orange, auburn, and gold. He would point to the antique country dining table and chairs and the plush plaid and floral couches and easy chairs in the living room. He would mention the soft goose down duvets on the beds and the weathered Adirondack chairs and rockers on the wraparound porch, where you could sit before dinner with your scotch and soda, listen to the crickets, and watch the fading light change the colors of the trees. He would single out Charlie Young, whose father had bought the eighteenth-century farmhouse in 1951 and converted it into what the ads in the island weekly extolled as "a destination for high quality food and a fine country living experience." He would tell them how Charlie's nightly ritual of ringing a cowbell to summon his guests to dinner—and then presiding at the head of the table, announcing each course on that night's menu, and proudly reading the label of each bottle of vintage wine he poured to accompany them—had been going on for decades.

But Felix knew all that would be lost on the new crowd. Yes, the inn was still full, but the guests now were younger, prettier, wealthier than his and Anna's old circle. They came not for Charlie Young's food and wine, or fine country living, but to disappear right after breakfast, driving off in their Jaguars and BMWs to make their tee times at the golf club where presidents played when visiting the island, or to the beach for sunbathing and windsurfing, or to town for a day of shopping. They returned at sundown, not to sit in the rocking chairs sipping cocktails, but to shower and change and then head out for dinner at one of the island's trendy new restaurants. Charlie Young still presided at the antique dining table, and still poured out the vintage wine, but there were now empty places every night and, most evenings, Felix was left to sit alone in the living room after dinner finishing that morning's *Times,* and then go to bed.

So why did he keep returning to the island year after year?

It wasn't for the cuisine or the ambience—not really. The truth was that Felix Goldman came back to the island to remember those long-ago summers—not only the golden Septembers with Anna at Hickory Hill House, but also those sun-drenched Julys and Augusts when the family rented cottages near the shore, those summers of long morning walks down the beach; building sandcastles, flying kites, and riding the waves with his children and then his grandchildren; angling for blues and stripers in Captain Gus's Boston Whaler, for him to grill on the charcoal barbeque or for Anna to put in one of her famous New England seafood stews.

Now, sitting on the beach alone was a bore, and he no longer had the strength to battle the surf. Old Captain Gus had sold the boat and retired—and, anyway, Felix doubted he could still reel in a keeper. So, all that remained of those times were the long morning walks.

With the turn of the new millennium, Charlie Young had put a computer in the library, where guests could read the news online. But despite the urgings of his children and grandchildren, Felix refused to read anything on a screen. So every morning, he would walk down the hill to the Mid-Island Country Store to buy the *New York Times.* He would get up at first light and put on his walking shoes. The inn would still be night-quiet, the living room deserted, the long dining table not yet set for breakfast, and the aroma of brewing coffee back in the kitchen still an hour away. He loved the early morning light even more than the dusk—the dew still wet on the grass, the morning songs of the sparrows, robins, wrens, and warblers, and the fresh salty breeze blowing in off the ocean. Some days, a family of deer, sunning themselves on the dirt road, would disappear into the woods as Felix approached.

Felix had been getting his *Times* at the country store for so many Septembers that Walter Hayes, the store's owner, kept Felix's copy for him behind the counter. Many mornings, the store had just opened when Felix got there and the *Times* hadn't even come in yet, so he'd chat with Walter about island gossip, or simply sip coffee on the porch until the papers arrived. Then, with the newspaper in hand, he'd head back up the hill in time for breakfast and the start of his day-long study of every page.

It was on these early morning walks that he would remember the island summers before Hickory Hill, when he had strength and stamina, and a lifetime in front of him.

He remembered the day their sandcastle turned into an excavation large enough to bury both of his daughters and one of their summer playmates in sand. Somewhere, Felix still had the photo Anna took of him leaning on a shovel next to three giggling, suntanned faces just sticking up, the white foam and blue ocean behind them.

He thought of the morning he set off down the beach after breakfast, knowing that if he kept walking, he'd arrive at the nude beach and be able to pretend he didn't know what it was, before turning back in mock embarrassment, but guilty satisfaction.

And then there was the time he invited a young business colleague and his beautiful blonde wife to join him for a day of fishing—a day he and Captain Gus knew was perfect for catching blues despite the brisk wind and whitecaps on the water. Soon after the Whaler hit open ocean, his young guests had succumbed to the three-foot swells. Seeing their faces turn pale, Felix told the old captain to turn around and head back to calmer waters, ignoring his protestations that they'd "never catch anything back in the harbor." He smiled as he recalled how they had still taken in more than a dozen blues and even an albacore.

Most of all, he remembered the long summer evenings after the girls were in bed, when he and Anna would sit outside in rocking chairs listening to the surf in the fading light, not saying anything, just being alone together.

He remembered all these things and more on his long morning strolls at Hickory Hill House. But Sundays were different.

On Sundays, rather than sleeping late like the rest of the guests, Felix got up a bit earlier, and walked down the hill a bit faster, to buy the Sunday *Times*. Although lugging the heavy Sunday paper back up the hill was becoming more difficult, and he often had to stop to catch his breath, he was driven by delicious anticipation of Charlie's famous Sunday brunch buffet—toasted bagels with smoked Scotch salmon and sable, perfectly cooked scrambled eggs with bacon and country sausage, hot waffles with pure maple syrup from the island—then the newspaper and, above all, the Sunday crossword puzzle.

•••

Now, after getting Charlie Young's news that Monday evening, Felix put the unfinished puzzle aside, and started thinking about Lynne and Robert. His morning walks those next few days were not about the past, but all about the expected new arrivals.

And then, on Friday morning, as Felix sat on the sunlit porch awaiting breakfast, with the *Times* spread out on his lap, there he was. He was balder and heavier than Felix had remembered, but the familiar blue eyes twinkled and he flashed the familiar smile.

"I'm Robert," he said, holding out his hand.

"Felix," he replied, getting up and grasping the hand firmly. "Pleased to meet you."

"Marvelous morning, isn't it? Mind if I borrow a section of your *Times* before breakfast? Charlie Young didn't tell us we could order the *Times* here."

"You can't. I walk down the hill to get it every morning," Felix said as he held out the three sections he wasn't reading. "Please, take your pick."

So they sat together on the porch, passing the newspaper sections back and forth, and when breakfast was announced, they went in and sat together. They talked about the glorious early fall weather on the island, the *Times'* coverage of the election and its review of the play that had opened on Broadway the previous evening, and the day ahead. As Charlie had requested, Felix offered to show him around Hickory Hill. "It's 56 acres, and you can easily get lost in the woods if you don't know which paths to take," he confided.

They agreed to meet before lunch for a walk, during which Felix identified each of the trees by its leaves and each bird by its song, and also might have mentioned the rented cottages near the shore, or Captain Gus, or sandcastles on the beach—or maybe all of them—which led to lunch together. Sometime between the New England clam chowder and the Nicoise salad, Robert told Felix about Lynne's new Off-Broadway play.

"She always used to pull an all-day disappearing act like this when she was learning a part," he confided as they parted after lunch, "but she hasn't done a new play in some time, so she's a bit nervous about memorizing her lines. Still, I'm sure she'll emerge for dinner," he said. "She'll enjoy meeting you."

Maybe it was the wine (Felix was sure Charlie Young had chosen his best Bordeaux to honor his special guests), maybe it was his surprise at how stunning she still looked (the red curly hair he remembered had now gone gray, but she still had Anna's piercing green eyes), or maybe it was just the thrill of being with them, but Felix was captivated. They talked about Broadway in the old days, when producers didn't need to miscast TV or film stars in order to draw audiences. He was excited to learn that they were opera-goers, and so they discussed the upcoming season and whether Peter Gelb was good for the Met. All three of them were hopeful that Obama would win the election and go on to do great things.

Over dessert, Felix recalled the first time he'd seen them together on the stage.

"Wasn't it *Uncle Vanya*?" Felix ventured.

"Chekhov, yes," she laughed, "but it was *The Cherry Orchard.*"

"That was more than forty years ago, Lynne," added Robert. "If you can remember that, you'll have no trouble learning these lines."

Then, pouring more wine, she confided how, even more years ago, she had stayed at an inn much like this one while preparing for a summer stock production of *Streetcar*. While she sat in bed at night reciting Blanche Dubois's passionate lines, the man beside her— "not *him*," she added, pointing at Robert—leaned over and asked, "Does this Blanche person like sex?"

Felix was sure Lynne didn't tell *that* story to just anyone.

More followed over cognac in the living room, but sooner than Felix wanted, it was "well, goodnight, look forward to seeing you in the morning." Felix rose to say goodnight, convinced this was the most agreeable evening he'd spent since Anna's death.

As they approached the living room door, Lynne turned around.

"Oh, Felix," she said. "By Sunday, I think I might be ready to start reciting my lines with someone reading the other parts. It never works with him," she added, giving her husband a knowing glance. "Do you think you could spare a few hours to read with me?"

Could he? "Of course," he managed to blurt out. "I'd be delighted."

As he tried in vain to fall asleep that night under the soft duvet, Felix thought of little else than seeing Robert in the morning to share the *Times,* of another walk (maybe even down to the beach), of her joining them again for dinner—and then of Sunday, reading lines while looking into Lynne's green eyes—her eyes, not Anna's. Lynne and Robert weren't just casual Hickory Hill House acquaintances, he told himself. They were becoming friends. They'd exchange phone numbers, have dinner at restaurants in the city, go to the theatre and opera together. In fact, as her script reader, he was sure he'd be invited to her opening night.

So, Saturday morning before breakfast, there sat Felix on the big porch with his *New York Times* and, yes, Robert soon appeared, said "Good morning. Sleep well?" and gladly accepted a section of the paper. No need for polite banter this morning—they were beyond that. And yes, they walked again that morning, all the way down to the beach, for the day was sunny and unusually warm for September. They talked more about opera, politics, the Middle East, so heedless of the time that they were late for lunch and had to eat hurriedly before the buffet was cleared away.

"Oh, I meant to mention this morning," Robert said as they parted, "we won't be here for dinner tonight." It seemed that Charlie Young couldn't resist talking around the island about his celebrity guests, so they'd been invited to a dinner party at the summer home of a prominent theatrical lawyer they'd known for years. There'd be lots of theatre people, he supposed. "We just couldn't say no," he explained, "but we'll see you tomorrow. She's still counting on you to read the script with her."

The rest of the day, and Saturday night, seemed empty to Felix. They had just met, so how could he already miss their company so much? How could he return to the solitude he'd come to accept since Anna's death? But he consoled himself with thoughts of the Sunday to come. She would get up for the sumptuous brunch. They'd pass the Sunday *Times* around three ways. The three of them would take a walk. And in the afternoon, he'd read with her.

Then, in bed that night, the thought came to him. He'd bet one of them was also a devotee of the crossword puzzle. And wasn't tomorrow the September Sunday when the Arts section came in four parts—previewing the new season in films, plays, music, opera, and dance? Why did they have to share his *Times*? The next morning, he'd buy *two* copies at the country store and present one to them, as a token of their new friendship.

Felix was up early Sunday, pulling on a wool sweater against the morning chill. But as the sun rose while he sauntered down the dirt road, eager to acquire the gift he would bestow, he realized that it was going to be another warm day—warmer than yesterday. Even before he reached the country store, the sweater had come off and was tied around his waist. Trickles of sweat began to run down his face. The *Times* delivery was late that morning, and Walter Hayes had taken the day off, so Felix sat on the porch in the sun waiting.

It was nearly nine before he was on his way back to Hickory Hill House, toting a shopping bag containing two copies of the *Times,* extra fat this Sunday because of the expanded Arts section. His load was heavier than he'd anticipated—much heavier, he had to say. And he'd have to hurry if he was going to reach the inn in time to present his gift before brunch. As he quickened his step, the sweat mixed with the sunlight in his eyes. He wiped his eyes with one hand, while he shifted the heavy shopping bag to the other. He realized how hard he was breathing and knew he should stop to rest, but he pushed himself on. He ignored the stitch developing in his left side. He didn't notice when the sweater around his waist fell to the ground behind him.

Finally, a little before ten, his face flushed and his shirt soaked in the back and under his arms, Felix staggered up the steps and slumped heavily into one of the Adirondack chairs, dropping his shopping bag on the next chair. Still panting, he pulled out his handkerchief and wiped his brow, then carefully unpacked the bag, putting one copy of the *Times* on his lap and arranging the other prominently on the next chair. He unfolded the front page and started to glance at the headlines. But within a minute, his chin dropped to his chest and his eyes closed. His *Times* slid from his lap to the floor.

He awoke suddenly to find Charlie Young's hand on his shoulder, gently shaking him.

"Felix! Are you all right? You gave me a fright for a minute."

"Oh. I must have... Don't worry. I'm fine." But Felix wasn't so sure; he'd given himself a fright, too.

"Well, come on in then. Brunch is almost over."

Then Felix noticed the second copy of the *Times* still folded neatly on the next chair.

"Where is... where are...? Lynne and Robert—did they go in to brunch without me?"

"Oh, them? No, they had to leave early this morning. Some emergency with the granddaughter at school."

"They're coming back, though, aren't they?"

"Well I hope so," said Charlie with a shrug. "I said I'd be glad to have them with us again next year."

Felix was dumbfounded. "Next *year?*" he gasped. "Not until next year?"

"Sure," Charlie replied. "I think they liked it here, but we'll have to wait and see. Having clients like that is good for my business, so I hope to see them back again next September."

Felix got up slowly and followed Charlie Young into the dining room. What about their walks? What about reading lines together? They hadn't even had a chance to exchange phone numbers. Was that it, all there would be?

Charlie had said he hoped Lynne and Robert would be back at Hickory Hill House next September. Felix hoped so, too. He was sure he would be back, but in the meantime, he might call one or two old friends in the city and suggest lunch. Then, too, he could start accepting some of those dinner party invitations he'd been refusing since Anna's death. And was it really so awful to buy a single ticket for the theatre? Maybe even to see a certain Off-Broadway play set to open next month?

Yes, Felix Goldman was sure he would return to Hickory Hill House next September. But maybe by next year, there might be someone to come with him. It didn't even have to be someone with green eyes.

Jan Steckel

When Fire Loved Water

Fire raged through a wood. He didn't know why he raged; it just seemed the thing to do. Bark crackled curling in his path; pinecones exploded. At first he didn't even realize he had come to a stop. It all just got quieter and clearer. A wisp of steam rose in the air. Before him sparkled a pool of Water, silver-blue in the sun. The Water rippled at him, laughing. His flame diminished, then burst out anew higher and hotter. He had no idea what had happened to him. He couldn't move forward, but he felt more alive than he ever had.

He reached out to the Water with one orange-gold flame, but as it touched her, it sizzled and went out. A small cloud of mist rose from the spot, only to disappear in the breeze. Once Fire had touched Water, he knew he could never leave, but neither could he embrace her. So he stayed on the edge of the pool, longing for what he could not have. All day and all night he burned there. He, who was used to consuming whole forests, was now himself consumed with desire.

When the sun rose behind the trees on the other side of the Water, Fire had burned himself down to nothing but a tiny flame. He barely heard the crunch of roughly shod feet approaching through the unburned undergrowth in the east. In the morning light, a man stepped from the trees and walked toward the pool. The man had killed a rabbit, which he set down on the grass of the bank. He carried a pouch of dried bilberries, and tied on his hip was a small aurochs-skin bag of rare oil. He meant to mix some of the oil with ochre and some with charcoal when he got home. He was thinking about how to paint a rabbit inside a cave so it would appear to run in flickering light. The Water seemed to sparkle for him, too. He took a step toward the pool, meaning to splash his sweaty face and slake his thirst.

The rabbit carcass burst into flame, sending the man staggering. "Man!" roared the Fire, "Pour your oil on the Water."

The oil was from a land far away. The man did not want to pour it out, but he could feel the heat of the Fire on his face and arms. Reluctantly he untied the little bag and emptied it into the pool. As the oil spread on the Water's surface, Fire moved down the bank. He sent tendrils of flame onto the oil, and at once spread onto it entirely.

Water felt the flames licking her, and sent up a cloud of mist. She enveloped Fire in a steamy embrace. For a moment, he burned so brightly that the sky itself flamed red and gold. Then, as the last of the oil burned away, she engulfed him, leaving only a hissing sound and a cloud of vapor.

The man told the story of Fire and Water over many a cooking-fire. His children told it to their children, who told it to theirs. Millennia passed, and snow and ice covered the land. The forest retreated. The men left, and many generations later, returned. In the land of Ice, though, even today, Water is hot, and the springs still boil with the heat of Fire.

Jan Steckel

Cut Out in Little Stars

The poet-musician Arion of Lesbos sailed home to show off the riches of popular success. Sailors coveted his gold and silver. They made him choose between a quick death and walking the plank. He asked for time to sing one song, so beautiful the dolphins swam over to listen.

   The cabin boy wept when Arion stepped off the deck and plunged a fathom or two into the Aegean, expecting to meet the Ferryman without boat fare. Down, down he sank. Water pressed against his eardrums and brine filled his eyes and nose and mouth, when in the dark salt wet he felt a wide slickness come between his thighs, thrusting him upward toward a watery sun.

   Mantle on shoulders and lyre in hand, he rode the dolphin's back all the way to Corinth, where he told the tyrant Periander his adventures, so rapt in his tale he failed to return the dolphin to the sea. His savior gasped its last upon the land while Arion sang enthusiastically of its heroics. Periander buried the creature in a monument.

   The sailors told the king that Arion died of a fever and no one could save him, so they had to bury him at sea. Voilà, out stepped Arion alive, alive-o from behind the dolphin's tomb. Periander crucified the sailors. (Don't you love a happy ending?)

   Apollo, who loved Arion, turned him and the dolphin into constellations. Handsome payment for a single song, but dolphins were men before they were fish, and as Richie Valens and Buddy Holly know, gods still covet the company of rock stars.

Anders M. Svenning

Comedy Ephtiakrivos

My *Giagia* Althea told me the upstate rivers were congested with *skata*. Mercury, garbage, and things that would make your baby's skin turn green, or have them grow a tail or a third eye, maybe. She said that. She said I was different and if I tried I could see jewels in the concrete and in the rusted fences. She told me each acorn on the ground was a treasure, and I avoided stepping on them.

Once, in this time, the sky outside the walls of Public School 105 cackled and spit, as it did on many a late-autumn afternoon in the city.

On the corner of Public School 105, our classroom gave onto tall windows standing clear on two sides, where the rain fell. Droplets pat-patting on the geometric windowpanes gave the room a sort of bountiful, greenhouse effect, and our class felt pushed to grow, aspiring in reaching the balls of light and gas that hovered above us at nighttime, the lights we all shared. We shared our lunches with one another—corn chips and sliced apples and peanut butter. We shared all the words, speaking a half a dozen languages and even the words we should not have shared, the bad words, which my Giagia Althea said made hair grow on your tongue if you said them.

It was a quarter of four and the class was clustered around our massive oak doorway, which gave into Public School 105's wheat-colored halls. "The bell does not excuse us. I do," Ms. Thurgood said, standing in front of the blackboard, looking young and virile in the light and sound.

To push open that door! Solid as aquarium glass, it was always moist to the touch, oiled and heavy in the sense that it and its brothers and sisters never had me understand the differences between our childhoods and what Ms. Thurgood called our potential soaring. It was the threshold—our door—smelling of earth, filling me with trodden maturity, knowledge, and sureness, the threshold between youthfulness and growth.

Even on days when it was not raining the school smelled musty in the upper levels of the staircases and in the elevator's carpet and metal, but on rainy days such as this, in some corners or inside the building's elevators, it was like a day at the Falls. You rubbed in the mist and were awoken.

Public School 105 was a good place. "Best junior high in the state," Giagia Althea, that is Grandma Althea, had said, and it felt good, being part of the greatest school in the tri-county area. The school, a mere few blocks from the house, was blocks and blocks down Eighth Street and a short scoot over on Fifth Avenue. Walking back, you get to the corner of Ninth, and there was home. The upstairs apartment was ours—

though the apartment was not small by city standards, it would not be fitting to call it lavish either—and Giagia Althea lived on the first level.

More often than not, I spent my time there, talking and eating with her, listening to age-old Greek wives' tales and her seemingly endless wealth of stories from the motherland. It was something to look forward to, spending time with her after school, and eating and playing cards.

The bell rang, and Ms. Thurgood released us, as if there were any difference between the two, and the three friends—Randy, Oba, and I—stepped out into what was becoming a sun-shower.

"It's clearing up, huh?" said Oba, stating the obvious once again, as he always did, and Randy firing back, "Sure is. It was almost darker than you earlier, Oba."

Oba was a quiet kid, Nigerian and full of wit. Really, there were not many times when he was not witty, spitting jokes and one-liners that kept our bellies aching. It was such an aspect of Oba that, when he was quiet, an infrequent occurrence, procured your always knowing he was there. "You know, Randy," he said, "you shouldn't talk so much. It makes you look confused. The way one eyebrow goes higher than the other, and your upper lip shows all your front teeth."

"Aww, snuff it," said Randy. And Randy, Randy, as peculiar as he was, was essential to the triangle. He kept us in a good spot, kept us going, wondering about things we never otherwise would have wondered. Randy could start a conversation, but could not finish it. It was like that Shel Silverstein illustration of *Where the Sidewalk Ends.* Many times, our conversation, no matter what it was about, would just drop off into a void of silence, and Oba and I would wait there with our eyebrows raised for him to say something more, but he almost never did.

Those two, Oba and Randy, were on their way to Randy's house. It was like a Wednesday evening ritual. They would go over to Randy's and look at the same picture of a girl wearing pasties, and comment with their most risqué raillery, unloading quips, whistling and shouting until their voices got scratchy, or they got hungry. Randy's sister was a photographer who had a rather bizarre flare when it came to her artwork.

Oba had an alibi, otherwise known as Salvation Army volunteer hours. He told Mama Oba that they liked him over there, and that he got free dinners. But really, he would go over to Randy's and eat bologna sandwiches and watch *The Price is Right* and play with the dog and get his belly tickled by such a girl in all her photogeneity. We stumbled across the pictures a while back, behind a burnt-out television in Randy's basement, thrown helter-skelter into two shoeboxes. The photos were labeled, *1996,* in red magic marker that had become a mellow orange. Porcelain bathtubs filled with water, milk cartons stacked high, a pair of feet, an alley with hung-out-to-dry T-shirts, which rippled overhead like flags outside the United Nations, and of course, our precious girl—all of which were in black and white—but, "It wasn't until after she started eating mushrooms when she got weird," Randy told me. I did not get it—how eating mushrooms could make you weird. We would always eat them at our house, for dinner, but I just nodded, and said, "Ohh," as if it was obvious what he meant.

That was another thing she said, my Giagia Althea. "Mushrooms help against arthritis, Dimi. Eat up and your knuckles won't hurt like mine when you're old like me."

It was common knowledge. Mushrooms were good for arthritis, just like corn on the cob was good for clearing acne. It did not matter. As long as she kept cooking, I went to sleep, under a food coma, and with our game of five-card draw, the diamonds, the hearts, the clubs, and the spades, coloring my dreams.

•••

Giagia Althea had come sometime after the Greek civil war, immigrated to Ellis Island during the late 1950s. She was an animated woman and spoke her mind, an animated woman in the most special case when she talked about the war, which had taken place between the communists and the capitalists, or the *malakes* and the *arnakia,* the shitters versus the lambs, translated to English. She mentioned once that the reason she took so radical a stance was because the commies had held a gun to her father's head and had scared the family halfway to Hades.

I was intrigued and asked her to tell me the whole story.

My Giagia said that her old man had spoken out against the Red militia one evening, at the village *taverna.* A little too much ouzo had loosened his tongue, and it was not long before the militia's supporters came to his house, put the man on his knees on the front lawn, and told him to pray to God.

"All six kids and my mother were watching," Giagia Althea said, her eyes slits. "Mama was screaming something, something about how her husband was good for the town, how he was a good person. All the kids were behind our mother—all except Voula, the second youngest, who you never got to meet before she died. She was pulling at our father's collar, trying to pick him up off his knees and get him back into the house. He made a promise that night," she said, "to himself as well as to the ones, you know, with the gun—he stopped talking politics, stopped supporting our side." My great-grandfather had lived through the dance.

Giagia Althea said God saved him, but my guess was that they were just trying to scare him bad. That was one of her many stories. It was captivating, listening to her talk about the people from before—icons in the eyes of the time-wary youth. It must have been the way she told them, in the Greek language, with the smell of garlic and thyme frying on the stove, somehow underscoring the stories' authenticity, which made me feel as if they were legends.

•••

The rain had picked up. Never-ending brick apartment buildings and cars parallel and double-parked lined the sides of the street. We had just crossed Third Avenue into a familiar neighborhood, a residential area, which had a few shops placed here and there like checkpoints: mom-and-pop delis, outdoor grocery stores, everything-shops where you could get anything from a gallon of milk to a *Penthouse*.

The three of us were passing one of these shops. It was a place we all knew by its phosphorescent yellow awning and green letters. Only now, underneath it, a man who I had never seen before, was sitting. Sheltered from the rain, he was flipping through a magazine, legs crossed and motionless. He turned to look at us and when our eyes locked, he said, "Ahh, boys! I know what you like, eh? A little something for your girlfriends? You come inside, eh? It's cheap for you. I've got to get rid of this stuff, you know?" The man's hair was dark, coarse, and slicked back.

"Why not?" Oba said. "Sure, we'll come in! Cheap stuff, right?"

"Sure, sure. Cheap, man. I'm telling you."

Under the awning we walked, past the fold-up chair on which the man had been sitting and through the open doorway, cracked and painted, and were accosted by the grime on the floor.

"Cheap!" the man yelled.

The place was spacious on the left-hand side when we walked in and a white wall was at our right shoulder. The shop could not have been more than ten feet wide, racks of potato chips hugging the right-hand wall a few feet further in, a narrow aisle crammed with paper towels, Windex, and washer detergent across from the potato chips.

"Cheap, man, I'm telling you," said the Persian, now behind the counter. He was pulling out a tray of shimmering watches and jewelry. "Ten bucks for the watches. Everything else, five dollars."

We began sorting through the jewelry, dividing the good stuff up from the bad, picking through the pieces—the rings, the watches, the bracelets, and the necklaces— and it all felt somehow undermining, I later realized, though I could not quite place the subtle feeling at the time. Undermining in the sense that moments ago we had been at ease, and now we were folded into a category of people who were, to this man, ripe for the plucking, and I remember there thinking of Giagia Althea, her father, and the commies.

The Persian, who I assumed was the owner, started talking to an employee, his son or nephew by the looks of him. The younger employee's face was in a grimace. He was helping a derelict-looking guy playing scratch-off lotto.

Bowling shoes were strapped to this derelict's feet; the olive-green sweatpants he wore looked like a boxer's. He was talking—monologuing, in all reality—to the clerk, with as much rationality as a flat basketball. "It's really something, huh?" he said. "Back in the day, when I could get into casinos, I played that roulette table like it was a goddamn cello. Made lots of money. Lost some, too, but made lots. Shit, this one's a loser. Get me another Monopoly. But, yes, I made money. It ain't no big thing. Casinos nowadays are fixed, though. House always wins. I'd stay away from those places if I were you. But if you want to go, you know, go for it."

At this point, the Persian's adrenaline seemed to be shooting up at the prospect of selling his fake Rolexes. I could see it in his eyes, felt it in the way he sucked the air into his lungs, as if the oxygen were running out. "So," he said. "What you guys think? Good stuff, eh?"

"Yeah, it's good stuff," said Oba. "How much for this one?" He held up a gold Rolex with a white face.

"Ten bucks." The Persian was trying hard to keep his face placid.

"Ten bucks, huh?"

"Ten bucks."

My ears were thrumming, and I made my proposition. "How about two for sixteen? I have an eye for that silver one."

"Two for sixteen, eh? I think I can do that. Okay. Two for sixteen!"

Oba and I put our money together. I had a five and three singles. Oba had a ten, and got two singles back as change, and not three minutes later we were walking out of the gritty shop with two watches sliding down our wrists—the Rolex on his and a Cartier on mine—thinking what a deal we just got, breathing in the fumes of our youthful effluence, which had somehow grown heavier as we walked our way further down Eighth Street.

I was her *Athanatos,* right out of my mother's womb. If her antics were any representation of her feelings, it would not be too crazy to have thought Giagia Althea took credit for my being alive. It was not just her *kotopoulo,* boiled potatoes, and powdered cookies that kept me alive and healthy. It was the fastidious tightrope balance between good and bad luck; superstition, it seemed, held elder Greeks captive like Riker's Island held the bad boys of Brooklyn. A little saliva on the forehead was good against the evil eye. Cracking hard-boiled eggs, first at their corners, then around their bellies, quelled bad blood between people. Coffee cups, too, had a mysterious equivocality.

I had grown up with these antics, suspension of action until the coffee cup was consulted. So, when Giagia Althea offered to read my coffee cup one night, it was not a portentous event. It was only another one of those intimate relationships between the deity that was future, and us.

It was a calm night, one of those nights when you feel relaxed and giddy simul - taneously. A white coffee cup was set upside down on the plate on which she had served it. The white coffee cup was set upside down to allow all the residue to find its way to the top of the white coffee cup. This was not your American coffee. This was Greek coffee, which was granular and relevant, and when you drank your way to the bottom of the cup, at hand were residual timestuffs that made a regular cup of Greek coffee into a decipherable fortune, like NASDAQ: AAP and the Nuestra España Fleet, but more accurate to Greeks.

She had made the coffee on the stove, her hair already in its curlers, and the innate streaks of perspiration glimmered on the nape of her neck, as they always had, because there was no such thing as a coffee machine in backcountry Greece and the old ways had followed her into the twentieth century, where we were talking about that which was important and also of those that are ignorable at best, passing the hours until Mom got home from the office where she worked, talking about school in general, but with more specificity we were talking about those who are of importance and who are known as girls; before all of which, we talked about luck.

"You think you're a lucky kid, Dimi?" That is short for Dimitri.

"Lucky?" I said. "Yeah, sure, Giagia. I think I'm lucky. Why not?"

"Good, good," she said. She had a way about her, a confidentiality that made that which was the matter substantial and believable. The coffee cup was another example of her self-proclaimed prescience, and while she was washing dishes in the kitchen and cleaning the countertops, she said, "You know what, Dimi? I'm going to make you a coffee." Five minutes later, she was pouring fresh brew into two cups, and then coming over to sit with me. "Enjoy," she said, sitting down in a chair, and then slurping on her coffee cup. She said. "Let it cool off, Dimi."

I did, and after a minute or two I took a small drink.

"It's good for you, Dimi. Drink it. One cup a day will make you live a long time."

"It's good," I lied.

"So, Dimi, you have your eye on any girls at school? Tell me."

This hit me and was rather awkward—I was not ready for such a question—because I was a timid person then and had not really come to terms with the elementary urges in my loins, but I told her the truth in any case: "Yeah," I said. "There's a girl named Jackie at school. I think she likes me. I hope she likes me," I said, and I told her that Jackie's eye had caught mine only a few times and that the first time had been for only a second and that our eyes met and she had pulled her eyes from my own, and I had felt an affection, and that the second time, our eyes dwelt on each other's eyes, and I could feel my stomach give out like the tympani.

"Dimi, you should talk to her. Dimi, I know what we can do. We'll read your *tychi*. We'll see what we can do about your girlfriend."

She looked under my overturned coffee cup. I was waiting for her to say something like "Hmm... interesting" or "Well, would you look at that," something cryptic, but she never did and, instead, looked at the streaks of liquefied coffee grinds, her face contorted in concentration as if she were deciphering the mountain.

"Dimi," she said, flat. "You know what this says?" She turned the coffee cup towards me. Dark brown stripes ran along its insides, touching, turning, and crossing each other in what was the fabric of the future.

"What does it say?"

"It says if you talk to that girl, you will have a long friendship together. It says it right here. Look. See? You have long roads. See? They'll carry you to good places."

I nodded.

"You talk to her, Dimi. Okay?"

"Okay, Giagia," I said.

"You want to watch TV?" she asked. "*To Tell the Truth* should be on. Come, Dimi." Giagia Althea got up and walked to the overstuffed couch, and we watched Garry Moore introduce me, myself, and I, to those on set, celebrity guests and spectators, and also to home viewers like you, and then when Mom arrived, as she always did at 9:00 p.m., she and I went upstairs to that not-so-small and not-so-lavish apartment, where I lay in bed and thought about Jackie and my *tychi,* and, very late, finally got to sleep.

•••

If there was any indication of how Jackie's dad would react to my interest in his daughter, I would have stopped short and cut the connection right there, but how could I have known of the *mpifteki* and its imminence at that point, in all regards?

It took me a few days to muster the courage, considered soon enough by he who, during lunch in 105's cafeteria, went over and sat next to Jackie Hopkins in one of those moments one could well call improvised. The cafeteria had its own whimsical fragrance—a mixture of tabletop disinfectant and chicken patties that were only seventy-five percent chicken and which, when corrugated with cheese, were quite lithe.

I had just picked up my sandwich from the lunch line and was walking through the layout of tables when I saw her auburn hair off to my left-hand side. It was good I had come late to lunch, otherwise I would have been sitting with Oba and Randy at our usual spot across the room, but Ms. Thurgood had asked me to take a slip of paper to Ms. Jesmine's room—"Room 302 on the third floor, don't take too long"—and so that meant going upstairs before heading down to lunch. But I did not mind, not at all, because wandering the halls of Public School 105 had turned into a pastime of mine towards the end of the previous school year, ever since I had turned a bit pococurante. Now, however, walking up to Jackie with a rallied-up mindset, pococurante was the farthest notion from my mind.

One-liners fired off in my head like arrows and left me incredulous. *Hey, beautiful. Let's make like rain and fall together. Your name must be Mickey, 'cus, girl, you blow my mind.* Cheeseball lines like that; cheesy enough to make the scenario in its entirety the answer to my problematic ideologies.

I was standing next to her now, looking into the shadows of her left ear. I must have looked like a *malakah* myself, just standing there for who knows how long, watching her, still as stone—I thought it was only for a second—until the girl Jackie was with stopped talking and looked at me, square, and said, "Hey, Dimi, what are you doing? Waiting for the bus?"

To which, I said, "I don't much like public transportation, but I ride anyway. Can I sit down?"

Jackie laughed, "Sure." She had spoken up, which was a good sign, and it would not be too long before sunshine and, as had been foreseen, the two of us would fall right into the crag, laughing and joking so much that at one point chocolate milk squirted from Jackie's nose, a procession which made us laugh even more, with tears running down our cheeks. The rest of the school day slid by with no exceptional happenings, besides the few times Jackie batted her eyelashes at me from across the room, like a super-model.

We huddled close to the oak door, in T-shirts and sweaters of all different colors, for Ms. Thurgood's word, because she was the bell. It was a sunny day with a sky like ragged jeans, letting through splashes of sunlight. Jackie said, "My dad should be outside. We walk home together. Don't embarrass me, okay?"

"J-whorl"—that was my name for her since lunch; I figured it would stick like paint on a wall, but it did not.

We walked out into the day, sunlight floating down from the clouds and pooling around people's ankles. He was hard to miss, standing against the chain-link fence with his arms and legs crossed. His rimless glasses sat low on the bridge of his nose, and there was a glare coming off of his bald, polished head.

Jackie introduced us, and his toothy smile spread large across his flawless face. Words were exchanged in a quick and lighthearted manner, and that was when I kissed his daughter on her cheek.

My feet left the pavement—I thought I was levitating a foot and a half off the ground, but in all actuality I was hanging by my collar—because the big man's arm was pressed against my neck and holding me off of the ground. Then he was telling me to "Find another girl for your experimenting with, you goddamn cranny ax!" He let me drop back to the ground, where I deftly regained my footing in a way I hoped would later make Jackie chortle. Then, they went away and I am sure J-whorl got an earful on the walk home. I took the long way back to the corner of Eighth.

Giagia Althea had been in the kitchen when I arrived, and I told her I had talked to Jackie. "How did it go?" she asked.

As if my stretched collar did not speak for itself, I told her what had happened, but withheld the newly conceived notion that her *tychi* reading had been wrong. Maybe she had made a mistake. Maybe the reading was damaged or compromised in some way—it was indeed possible, no?—and as I sat down at the kitchen table, with a glass of water, I realized that was what had happened.

I checked my brand-new Cartier, which read four-twenty, about twenty minutes past the time I got home after school. The three of us—Oba, Randy, and I—had made the short hop from Eighth to Ninth, and had broken up at the corner. Oba and Randy continued down Fifth Avenue as I hung the right onto my street, where towering oak trees stood, and I, between them, shuffled into our driveway and walked through to the small ten-by-fifteen slab of concrete called the backyard, where the backdoor to our house was located.

All Giagia Althea said when she saw me was, "Where you have been, Dimi? You're twenty minutes late."

"Giagia, it's okay," I said. "I stopped in the store to get something."

"Stopped in the store to get something," she said. "And what did you get?"

I pulled my hand from behind my back, and the shiny Cartier screamed total and understated class from my wrist. It looked damned stack, but she did not think so. She bit her lip, and looked at the watch as if it were the most heinous thing she had ever seen.

"Dimi, what is this?" she said, and paused. "What are you? A gangster or something? Where did you find this, Dimi? Tell me."

"I got it from a guy by the school, Giagia. Relax. It was cheap."

"Dimi, your Papou and I worked hard to buy this house," she said. "And you are going around buying this, this *skata*?" She said that last bit in Greek, so I knew she was quite serious.

"It was cheap, Giagia. Eight bucks. There's nothing to worry about."

"Dimi," she said. "I hate to do this, but you have to learn. You have to learn what's important in life. Come with me."

"Where are we going?"

"We're going right back to that store, Dimi, and we're going to get that money back and get rid of that—*thing*." She was wound up. "Come. You think I'm joking?"

So, I was walking up the street again, with Giagia Althea, towards the Persian's shop, where I would lose possession of this accessory if she had her way. By her speedy strut and confidence, I expected she would not relent until that happened. A bus coughed acrid smoke as it passed, its hydraulics sighing as if in sympathy, which was not the case.

We entered the residential neighborhood. "Here it is," I said. "This is the place." The fold-up chair was gone. I was at Giagia Althea's heels as she stormed into the place, blew past the potato chip rack, and set both hands on the countertop, asking for the guy who owned the place.

"It's me," said the Persian. "What do you want?" He glanced at me, and his eyes opened like dinner plates when he realized who it was.

"Did you sell this watch to my boy?" Giagia Althea asked. The Cartier was off my wrist and in her hand. She placed it on the counter and the Persian raised his eyebrows and tucked his elbows back, hands akimbo, and said, "So what if I did. It's a free country, and he's not a small child no more. He can buy these things if he wants."

"A free country? A free country? Don't you tell me what is best for my boy. There's nothing worse than a money-hungry—bug. And you know what? I want you to take this thing back," Giagia Althea said, pushing the watch towards him. "And give us our —how much was it, Dimi?"

"Eight."

"Give us our eight dollars back before things get so ugly in this place that you look good."

He watched her, dullness pulling at the corners of his mouth. "Lady, what do I look like? There are no returns."

I thought she was going to have a conniption.

"Okay, you listen here," she said. "I don't how much eight dollars is to you, but that money in my hand in under sixty seconds will save you a very hard time."

Another customer walked into the store and turned right back out onto the street.

The Persian wet his lips with his tongue, and grabbed the watch off the counter. "Woman, here's your eight dollars, but only because I want you out of my shop. Now." Eight dollars—a five and three singles—was scooped up and put into her purse, and again we were on the street.

"Dimi," she said, somewhere closer to home, "I don't want you going back to that place," and she left it at that.

Oba would be wearing his Rolex tomorrow, and he would ask me where my watch was. I would have to brush the truth with a loose lie, saying I only wore those kinds of high-class accessories for high-class occasions, and school was not at all high-class. He would laugh and agree.

Walking past the shop would be a cold reminder. I had hoped the Persian would not make a habit of sitting under the awning. For the second time that day, I looked at the Verrazano Bridge, hazy in the distance. It was a pernicious characteristic all people on Eighth Street seemed to enjoy, but, because of its normality, let slip from their minds.

I looked at the edifice—it did seem as though someone had painted it—with its suspension cables running up along its sides, all the way to where its peak played against the gray sky. Way up there I thought I saw something, a small fleck of a thing, circling.

An eagle, Giagia Althea once said, had its nest way up on top of that bridge. "If you ever see it, if you ever do, on any day at all, you know luck is following you through the streets. It's up there, Dimi. All you have to do is look."

The bridge's summit was far and inconsistent, clouds now moving and obscuring the wide panorama. I kept my eyes fixed on the spot I thought I had seen the bird, afraid to blink for fear of missing it. My eyes began to water and, just before letting my gaze fall back to the grimy and cracked sidewalk, I blinked back moisture at an empty sky. Giagia Althea was walking slow. I kept up with the clicks of her shoes. The clicks had fallen into rhythm with my own heartbeat, and that made me feel better, wholesome, grounded and connected with her. The sky, at the peak of that bridge, had begun to clear. The eagle was a negative iridescence, burned in through vision and expectation; but seeing it up there, circling, as if in search of its next meal, I realized, must have been only a temporary illusion cast from a languishing imagination.

Stephen John Walker

Danger Island

Pukapuka Atoll, the Cook Islands, 1938

"Harry, look at the bloody fools. Don't they know we're here?" McCombs said.

"Well…yes…maybe," the schooner captain answered.

"Maybe? They've got eyes, ain't they?"

"Well, Davie, you know how it is. They've been a long time without a ship, and—"

"Then why don't they come out, now we're here? Squattin' on the beach like a bunch of dummies. We've been standin' off since first light."

"They'll come along directly. Anyway, Alberti will." Captain Houchins reached for his binoculars.

"Alberti. He's nothing but a bloody *kanaka* now. Lost what little mind of a white man he had."

"Alberti? He's the trader, isn't he?" Reggie asked. "What's a *kanaka?*" Reggie Pobjoy, the eighteen-year-old cabin boy, and Tooks Marsten, the Maori first mate, stood behind the captain and the supercargo on the wheel deck. The young man remembered his father using that word, but never knew the meaning.

Tooks tapped Reggie on the shoulder and placed a finger to his lips and pointed to his ear.

"Quiet, laddie," the supercargo said over his shoulder. "Just watch and listen. Lots to be learned doin' that. Your questions will be answered in their own time."

"Alberti a *kanaka*? I wouldn't say that about all white men, Davie," Houchins said. "If you were alone here for months, years sometimes on end, the way Alberti is, never seeing a white face—"

"Me? Here? I wouldn't be such a damn fool. Didn't Auckland send a new resident agent out since we were here last? There's a white face for him."

"Resident agents. Ha! There isn't one of 'em but what is the two ends and a bight of…a scoundrel." The captain tossed his cigar butt over the fantail. "We should've had that cargo, but we were laid up in Whangarei." Houchins nodded towards the island. "There's Alberti now."

"Well, it's about bloody time," McCombs said.

Both men raised their binoculars. An outrigger came out from the center of the island and headed for the gap in the reef.

"Maybe you're spot on, Davie. Looks like Alberti's come unhinged."

The canoe approaching the reef had three native paddlers, but in the middle was a white man sitting upright in a chair fixed astraddle the gunwales. An umbrella, lashed to the back of the chair, shaded the white-suited, pith-helmeted occupant from the sun.

Doctor Dozier joined the others around the wheel. He looked a bit haggard. "These Cook Island girls are very demanding." The Frenchman smiled and added, "Medically speaking, *bien sûr.*" He placed his travel bag and a white box with Red Cross markings on the deck.

McCombs lowered his binoculars. "That's not Alberti. He's over there on the beach."

The others looked toward the shore, where a white man stood near the waterline waving his hat. Of average height, but quite thin and bare-footed, he wore shorts and an open shirt.

"Righto, lads. That's our man." The schooner captain removed his cap and waved at the trader.

A shout from the bowsprit turned the attention of those around the wheel back toward the canoe working its way through the reef opening. The canoe that was now upside down and its occupants swimming in the surf.

"Ha! That's one for the books, Davie, me boy. When's the last time you knew of a Pukapuka canoe capsizing in the gap? Something funny here." He turned to the first mate.

"Mister Marsten, the dinghy over the side, if you please. There's a good lad."

"Come, Reggie," Tooks said. "We go save the *Papa'ā.*"

• • •

After Reggie and the first mate pulled the white man into the dinghy, they rowed back to the schooner. The man patted his pockets and looked around in the surf. He shook his head.

"God almighty, I hate this place! Now I've lost my best pipe, my only decent tobacco, *and* my hat."

Looking over the man's shoulder as he rowed, Reggie watched the three island paddlers right the outrigger and start towards shore. One wore the agent's pith helmet.

• • •

When Tooks and Reggie helped the agent up the schooner's side, the captain, the supercargo, and the doctor didn't go forward to meet him. Soaked to the skin, the short, slightly obese and balding bureaucrat followed Reggie to the wheel deck.

"Elrod Swint, Resident Agent for Pukapuka, and the king's representative in these waters, thank you very much. Did you bring the doctor and the drugs? And what is the nature of your cargo?"

"I'll leave the formalities to you, Doctor. And Mister McCombs." The captain turned and walked to the fantail. He lit another cigar.

"*Bonjour,* Monsieur Swint. I am Doctor Claude Dozier with the *Polynesie Française* medical service." The Frenchman extended his hand. "I have the necessary serum for the vaccinations. How many cases are there?"

The agent squinted and looked the doctor up and down. He didn't take his hand. "A bloody Frog? Couldn't they send an English doctor?" He looked to the supercargo, who shrugged his shoulders.

"Welcome aboard, Mister Swint. I'm McCombs, the supercargo. How can I be of service?"

Doctor Dozier stepped forward between the two other men. "I must insist, Monsieur Swint. How many typhoid patients have been confirmed? Have they been isolated?" A head taller than Swint, thirty pounds heavier and quite fit, Dozier, both hands raised waist high, looked like he was about to toss the agent over the side.

Swint backed away. His expression of arrogance changed to one of fear. "Three. The island nurse is dealing with them...Monsieur Doctor. They're in a hut on the far end of the island. I want nothing to do with this."

The doctor turned to the captain, who'd been watching from the fantail. "Captain Houchins, I must go ashore immediately."

The captain strode forward and ordered, "Mister Marsten, lower the longboat. Reggie, help the doctor with his kit." Houchins took the doctor by the arm and led him to the ship's waist. He ignored the agent as he passed. Reggie grabbed the doctor's gear and followed.

Miffed by this slight, Swint turned his attention to the supercargo. "Your cargo, sir?" He put his hand to his head, and then patted his pockets again. "I can't believe I've lost my hat. I've had it since Calcutta. And my pipe—my favorite pipe." He looked over the side of the schooner. "All down there, I suppose."

"Mister Swint, sir. Not to worry. These are just minor inconveniences of life in the tropics. Do come below to my trade room, and we'll get everything sorted."

"But your cargo, sir. McCombs, is it? I'll need to see an inventory."

"Of course, Mister Swint, in good time. But first we must get you out of these wet clothes. And some warmth in your body." The supercargo escorted the resident agent below.

Back on deck, Reggie approached the captain. "Sir, may I ask a question?"

Captain Houchins didn't answer. He watched the crew lower the longboat over the side and puffed on his cigar. A big smile creased his face when he turned to Reggie.

"I'd give a guinea to be a speck on the wall below in the trade room right now, lad." He laughed. "Davie will be plying His Majesty's Resident Agent with cheap Flipo rum after offering him a new pipe and a bucket of *tabac*. And a new *chapeau*." He reached out and placed a hand on the boy's shoulder. "What's your question, lad?"

"Why didn't the islanders come out when we arrived?"

Oroa, one of the Pukapuka girls, came up from the trade room with Swint's wet clothes and laid them out on the main mast boom to dry.

"Ha! There's another one for the books, Reggie, me lad. Davie's got island lovelies undressing his nibs below decks."

Captain Houchins and the doctor climbed over the side and into the longboat, where four rowers waited. Reggie handed down the doctor's gear.

"Come aboard, lad. You should meet Alberti. I'll answer your question as we go to shore."

Reggie went over the side and sat in the bow of the longboat. Tooks stood above at the railing.

"You have the helm, Mister Marsten," the captain said to Tooks. "Allow no one aboard or ashore until we sort out this typhoid business. I'll return directly or send word." He turned to the rowers. "Push off."

The captain and the doctor sat in the stern sheets of the longboat on either side of the Maori helmsman. Houchins turned to the Frenchman.

"Are we in time, Doctor?"

"Perhaps, Captain," Claude Dozier said. "No one has died. I estimate we are in the third week of the disease. These are very healthy people, and the infected ones were isolated early on. I am most pleased that there is a nurse who seems to know what she is about. Unfettered, this could have spread throughout the entire population. Then there would have been a major problem."

The captain looked forward and remembered Reggie's query. "Your question, lad, about the Pukapukans not coming out to meet us."

Reggie nodded and smiled. *He remembered.*

"They're a strange lot, these Pukapukans. Trace their families from Samoa, not Tahiti. Never been able to sort them out, even though I can muddle through with their lingo." He paused for a moment. "What if a canoe capsizes in the reef passage, for example. The Pukapukans ashore would gaze at the people dashing about in the water and say, 'Look, their boat's capsized. They are in the water. It is something new. Well, it was their idea to go out there. Let's sit here and see how they get themselves out of the water.' It's not that they're uncharitable or self-centered or anything like that. Rather the reverse, in fact. It's just that the idea would never occur to them to do anything to help."

Captain Houchins threw his cigar butt away. "It's the same with our arrival. It's something new. 'Let's see if they're coming for a visit. Nothing to get excited about.'" He lit another cigar. "Strange lot these. At any other island, we'd have a hundred canoes around the *Wallaroo* before we dropped anchor."

•••

Under the power of the *Wallaroo*'s rowers, the longboat shot through the reef gap and was soon on the beach. A crowd surrounded the craft. Makea, the island's *ariki*, placed leis over the heads of the three white men. Doctor Dozier immediately recognized the nurse by her white cap, even though she wore a *pareu*. They hurried off toward the far end of the island. Two island men carried his bags.

The trader pushed his way through the crowd and greeted the captain with open arms.

"Well met, you ol' pirate," Albert Freshour said to Houchins. "Good voyage? I was hoping you'd get the contract. You're here sooner than I expected." They shook hands and then hugged. "Who's the kid?" He nodded at Reggie.

"My replacement. A stowaway out of Auckland, or was it Whangarei? Can't remember. He wants to be a copra schooner skipper, but we're doing what we must to push him out of it. Davie has him under his wing, so you know he'll be corrupted straight away." He turned to Reggie.

"Lad, meet a good friend, even if he's a Yank. Came to the islands a decade or more ago to write the great novel of the South Pacific, but he's not a bad lot and a good trader."

The American looked over their shoulders. "Where's Davie?"

"Still aboard. Entertaining your man Swint."

"Well, I hope you brought him lots of bully beef. He won't eat anything native."

"Not getting on well with this one then, are you, Alberti?" Houchins said.

"He's an ass, this one is," the trader said.

Some of the islanders started to slide outrigger canoes into the water. The captain turned to the *ariki*.

"Tell your lot no one goes aboard until the doctor gives the okay."

Makea walked away to talk to his people.

Reggie followed Houchins and Freshour up the white pebbled beach to a single-story building made of rough boards with an unpainted iron roof—the S. L. Livingston Company's store and warehouse, and the trader's home. It sat amongst the coconut palms and had a covered porch along its front.

"Won't even try to learn the language," Alberti continued. "Won't eat anything except what comes out of a tin. The village mamas offered him wonderful meals—fish, pig, all their best. He wouldn't have any of it." They walked up the steps to the porch and into the store. "So they brought it all to me. What a feast!"

When they entered the main room of the store, Reggie looked at the shelves behind the counter—canned goods, bolts of colorful cloth, kerosene lanterns, hatchets, saws, knives of various sizes, jars full of stick tobacco, a rack of umbrellas, and three Singer treadle sewing machines. And there were boxes of thread and sewing needles next to a line of brown beer bottles with wire-fastened porcelain stoppers. All like what he'd seen in the trade stores on other islands, except the beer.

"Welcome to the finest watering hole in this quadrant of the South Pacific," the trader said with widespread arms. "What'll you have?" He pointed to the bottles on the shelf. "We have some properly aged home brew, some not-so-old home brew, and a batch of new stuff."

Alberti walked behind the makeshift bar—a wooden plank lying across two stacks of packing boxes. Above his head hung a hand-lettered sign: *The Danger Island Cantina.* Makea joined them.

What's a cantina?

"That jerk even wanted to close down my bar."

Two islanders came into the store. The trader opened bottles for them. They laid some coins on the bar, which Alberti scooped up and examined. "Frog francs." He shook his head and dropped the money into a cigar box.

What's wrong with the coins?

Four small children, naked except for *pareus,* burst into the store and surrounded the schooner captain. Houchins thrust his hands into his pockets, and then held out closed fists to the urchins.

"Which hand?" he said smiling. The children paused for a moment. The oldest, a girl of maybe ten, pointed to his left hand. The five glass marbles in his palm disappeared in an instant, and the children flew out of the store to start their game. Houchins handed Alberti five marbles from his right hand. "For later," he said. "Davie has more aboard. How do they manage to lose 'em between visits?"

Alberti shrugged and laughed. "*Tamanu* seeds make a good substitute. Fancy a pickle?" He placed a large glass demi-john of green floating things on the bar. "Left over from the Battle of Verdun, I expect." No one took a pickle. "Got them off a Frog tramp steamer that passed through some months ago. That's probably where the francs came from." Alberti opened four bottles of the aged beer. "Let's go sit outside." He handed a beer to each of the others. Seated in comfortable chairs made of local materials, the trader continued his tirade about the resident agent.

"Didn't come for a visit until he'd been here two weeks or more. Don't think he likes the idea of me marrying an island girl and having a brood of half-breeds, as he called them." He took a drink from his beer. "It almost came to a head when he said that." The American stood and walked to the porch railing. "I've still got my old Colt .45 service revolver, and I almost thought about finishing him off." He took another pull on the bottle. "Could've dumped his body off the outer reef. No one the wiser."

He can't be serious. Kill a man for a slight like that?

Makea nodded, as if in approval, smiled at Reggie, and winked.

"Speaking of firearms, Alberti. What happened to the gun rack you had?" Houchins said, to change the subject.

"Full of umbrellas now. Got a few old Mausers and a shotgun or two stashed away in the warehouse. The Bible thumpers and Wellington bureaucrats don't cotton much to the idea of islanders being armed. The days of booze and guns are past, I'm afraid, Harry. Now, it's all sewing machines and canned goods."

"Well, Albert, my old friend, we'll have to live with these things. Did bring you some makings for your home brew though." Houchins stood and joined his friend at the railing. He lit a cigar and handed one to the trader. "Times are a changing. RAs come and go, and you've survived worse, I know." He lit Alberti's cigar. "They come with big dreams about how they'll change their world and it usually doesn't happen. Some do great things. Some are just lotus eaters, and some are just putting in the time until their pension. But, we have to live with them and their foibles. Mustn't let them interfere with our trade. Heard bad things about the Japs up north in the old German islands. Stopped all outside shipping. Some say they're building big military bases everywhere. Not good." He looked out to the lagoon. "Now, what's all this?"

A lone crew member of the *Wallaroo* was rowing the schooner's dinghy through the reef gap toward the beach.

"Reggie, my lad, go see what that's about."

"Aye, aye, sir," Reggie said, and went down to the beach to wait for the dinghy. Under one of the palm trees he passed two island girls who gave him big smiles. *Wonder if we're staying the night.*

Reggie pulled the dinghy up onto the beach. Tupai, the crew member, handed him a folded piece of paper—a note from McCombs: *Harry, I've got this Swint sod sorted. He won't be any bother. Can we come ashore or is the plague still rampaging amongst the natives?*

"Will you wait here, *inē,* Tupai?" Reggie said. "Must take it to the captain." The crewman nodded. Reggie felt uncomfortable giving orders to the crew—he was one of them. Even though he was a white man, he was still just a crew member. The rowers from the longboat remained on the beach, making new friends among the island girls. Tupai joined them.

As Reggie walked back up the beach he saw the palm groves around the store had filled with islanders. They weren't going into the store, just sitting under the trees and waiting. He'd been told by Davie that there were three villages on the island; the other *motus* around the lagoon only used to raise crops or coconut palms. To Reggie, it looked like everyone on the atoll had assembled at the store. He wondered why. The government office was in the middle village, not here.

The doctor came through the coconut grove next to the store and joined Reggie.

Dozier bounded up the steps to the porch. He smiled. "*Mes amis,* I think we have, how do you say, nipped it in the butt."

There was a pause, and then the others laughed, but not the *ariki,* who didn't understand the joke.

"So, a lot of needle jabs in their posterior parts, right, Doctor?" Alberti said.

"*Non. Dans le bras.* In the arm." He looked confused by their laughter. "Did I say something humorous?"

"Not to worry, Doctor," Houchins said. "We understand. What needs doing?" He read the note from the supercargo.

The doctor noticed the bottles in their hands. "Beer? *C'est bière?* Is that beer?"

"*Oui, Monsieur Docteur, c'est bière. Une bonne bière,*" Makea said. "A good Pukapukan beer."

"*Parlez-vous français, monsieur?*" Dozier asked the chief.

"*Un peu, Monsieur Docteur, mais l'anglais est…*easier for me."

Alberti went inside the store and took a well-aged brew off the shelf. Back on the porch, he opened the stopper and handed it to the Frenchman.

"*Merci beaucoup, monsieur.*" Dozier took a long pull on the bottle.

Houchins offered him a cigar. "How do we sort this out? The jabs, I mean. How can we be of assistance?" He lit the doctor's cigar.

"*Bien.* Monsieur Makea, I must have your people assemble at the government office in Roto village. There, Nurse Tupou and I will conduct an examination, administer the vaccinations, and complete the necessary paperwork. It is absolutely essential that every inhabitant of this atoll complete this procedure."

"Yes, I know this to be true. I must talk to my people first, Doctor," Makea said. He left the store and went out into the crowd among the coconut palms.

"He's a good man, Doctor," Alberti said. "Best to give him some time with his folks. They'll come around when they're ready."

"How long will this take to be done with?" the captain asked. "I need to be clear of Toka Reef before dark."

"We may finish today, *mon capitaine,* but I have my doubts. And there will be examinations for some time to determine if the disease has been stopped." He spread his hands and shrugged. "I must stay until the end, *n'est-ce pas?*"

"Well, the contract was just to deliver you here. How will you get on to Papeete then? We won't be returning for some months."

"A few days ago, there was a French navy warship nearing Tongareva—Penrhyn, as you call it—on a courtesy visit. I heard that on the wireless while aboard the clipper en route to Aitutaki. They heard some transmissions in French and asked me to translate. If Monsieur Swint can be persuaded to communicate with them via wireless, they may rescue me from this plague, if I word the message properly." He grinned.

"What about my boys? They've been on the beach for a bit and chatting up the local damsels, I'm sure. Do they need to be jabbed again?"

Non, mon capitaine. Your men are *bon,* as are you, *mon ami.*" He handed his empty bottle to Alberti. "*Maintenant,* now, I must go to work." He held out his hand. "*Bon voyage, mon capitaine.*" The doctor shook hands with the captain and Reggie. He held Reggie's hand for a moment and said, "Young man, you can do worse than learning from these men. They are honorable men. That's important in this world." With a wave of his hand, he jumped down the porch steps and ran to catch up with the flow of islanders heading toward the other village.

"Well, that's a Frenchie I could learn to like and respect," the trader said.

"He's a *pied-noir*—French, but born and raised in Algeria," Houchins said. "Understand they're looked down upon by the Parisians—French, but not quite French. Much as are our half-breed islanders. He was posted to Indo-China for some years before ending up in the islands. Only spent the days with him between Aitutaki and here, but he has a top spot in my log."

"You met him in Aitutaki? How'd that happen?" Alberti asked.

"The planets seemed to be in line for this one, mate, if you believe that rubbish." Houchins lit another cigar. "We'd just tied up at Rarotonga, and were off loading copra from the southern group when the commissioner came aboard in a rush and offered us a lovely sum to dash north to Aitutaki, pick up some typhoid drugs, and carry on to here. Ol' Rupp said he would weigh the cargo and pay us when we returned. We did take aboard some home brew makings for you, Alberti. Can't let an old friend down, right? And some cases of canned goods for Swint, now that I know his name."

"The drugs were at Aitutaki?" the trader asked. "How'd that come to be?"

"Remember what I said about the celestial bit? That Yank airline, Pan American, was doing a route survey, they called it, to open a new service for their flying boats from Sydney to Honolulu. Their clipper flew the typhoid drugs and Dozier from Auckland to Aitutaki, landing in the lagoon. They were waiting for us when we arrived. As quick as could be, we hauled anchor and beat north to you." The captain finished his beer and set the bottle on the railing. "Did pick up a couple of Pukapuka lovelies who needed passage home. Don't remember why they were that far south, but it didn't matter. They've kept the doctor and Davie entertained." He laughed.

"I've got some copra for you. Time to take it on board?"

"No, Alberti. Sorry, ol' friend. Need to be south of here as soon as possible. And as quick as can be. No extra ballast. We'll up anchor and be gone before dark. May make a quick call at Suwarrow along the way, but need to get to a safe anchorage—Aitutaki or Raro—before the cyclone season kicks in."

"Suwarrow is it?" Albert asked. "Still looking to find Mair's gold, are you now?"

"Right you are, mate. Always the chance a blow has uncovered something. Be lovely to stay longer, but needs must. Next time we'll let some barnacles grow on the anchor chains. We did bring you the makings, and Swint's Spam," he said again. "I'll send them along as soon as we are rid of your RA. Come, lad," he said to Reggie. "Time to go aboard."

"Can I ask a question, sir?"

The captain paused and put his hands in his pockets. "Haul away, lad."

Reggie turned to the trader. "Mister Alberti, what was wrong with those French coins? And would you really have shot the government man?"

Albert Freshour took a step back, shook his head and said, "You've got a deep one here, Harry." The trader went back to the bar and opened the cigar box. He took out some coins, returned to the porch, and handed them to Reggie.

"Some souvenirs from Danger Island. Your good captain will explain their value later." Freshour paused for a moment, and then said, "Would I have killed the ignorant *pommy* for his slur about my family? No, but the idea did raise some possibilities. No. I saw enough killing in France in '18. Those are very good questions, young man. You'll go far. If, of course, you don't spend too many years with this old pirate and his partner in crime, Davie McCombs."

• • •

Davie and Resident Agent Swint, who wore a new Panama hat, waited in the schooner's waist when Reggie and the captain returned in the longboat. Two outrigger canoes lay alongside. The two Pukapuka girls stood close to the supercargo.

"Mister Marsten, make to get underway," Houchins said to the mate. "Mister Swint, your kit will go in the canoes, along with yourself. No time to have my boats go and return. Weather's getting nasty. Must be away." He turned to Reggie and winked. "Stay close, lad. Have a special cargo for you."

The agent climbed over the side to one of the canoes. The girls joined him. They headed to shore.

The captain turned to the supercargo. "Right, Davie. What've we got for Alberti?"

"His makings, of course. A bag of marbles for the kids, cigars, and a couple cases of Gordon's. He does like his gin, even if he is a Yank. Some ammo for his Mausers and shotguns, and a box of books."

"A great reader, Alberti is," Houchins said. "Right. Over the side then, Reggie. The canoe will take his nibs to the center village, while you slip ashore close in and give Alberti his cargo. They'll secure it in the longboat as soon as Swint is off a bit."

They watched the islanders paddle through the reef and toward the center village. When the RA's canoe rounded the point, Reggie was away in the longboat. The supercargo stood at the rail and shouted, "No time for chitchat, laddie. Alberti will be waiting. Give him my regards, but drop your cargo and make speed back. We're getting underway."

The trader was at the waterline with two islanders when Reggie's rowers brought the longboat parallel to the beach. Alberti and the Pukapukas unloaded the cargo and pushed off the boat.

"Hope we meet again, Reggie," Alberti said. "Good luck treasure hunting."

•••

On the schooner, the sails were being hoisted as the longboat was brought on board. Reggie joined the captain and first mate at the wheel. The wind had increased in strength.

"I'll have a course heading of 270° until we clear Toka Reef, Mister Marsten, if you please," Houchins said. "Reggie, me lad, a lesson for you. See that smudge of a sandbar off the port bow?"

Reggie could barely make out a white gleam in the choppy sea.

"That's the west end of Toka Reef. It runs pretty near four miles out from Motu Kotawa. That's that bit of island with the palms further along the lagoon." He pointed to the south with his cigar. "Many a not-so-bright skipper has gone aground there. That's why Pukapuka is also known as Danger Island. We always give it a wide berth, and never try to close on the lagoon's passage at night." He lit his cigar. "It's best to lie off to the west and make landfall at first light."

The *Wallaroo* heeled to port as it sailed close-hauled away from the atoll.

•••

Matt Whelihan

Cow

I was twenty-one miles into a marathon outside of Cooperstown. The temperature had just breached 90 and my legs had just decided they could no longer support my weight or keep me moving in a straight line. Without them to rely on, it was no longer a physical feat, just a mental one.

I was trying to keep myself from looking down the road ahead of me, to keep my eyes from the slowly approaching hill, the one that was sure to turn my slow jog into a slower walk. Instead, I looked at some farmland to my left and a house with stained siding to my right. There was a pile of old radiators on its lawn, like the kind that had hissed through the winters at my elementary school.

I was talking to myself at that point, a sign that my brain was getting closer to the state of my legs. But I wasn't saying anything outlandish yet. Just "Come on" and "So close." It was a failed pep talk; an effort that only reminded me I had hangover-level dry mouth.

And then I saw the cows.

There were ten or fifteen of them behind a simple, wire fence, munching in the shade of some trees. Maybe they were superb examples of their species, maybe blood flow had been diverted to my legs, leaving my brain without enough oxygen, or maybe I just wanted to avoid the hill, but those cows were important at that moment, important enough for me to slow to a limping walk and eventually a complete stop.

They groaned, but ignored me, and I noticed that they all had numbered tags attached to an ear.

I stared at the closest of the bunch. It was white with brown blotches. Its tail swished, its ears twitched, and it exposed its gums each time it chewed. When I read the number on its tag, I started to laugh. In my mind, I had just crafted the best joke ever.

I removed my phone from my armband and took a picture of the cow, making sure that the number on the tag was visible. The joke wouldn't work without that 187.

I opened Facebook, clicked the option for a post, selected the photo of the cow, and then typed: *187 on a motherfuckin COW.* I pressed submit, still giggling like a kid hiding a prank from his mom, and then I put the phone back in the armband. It was time to finish the marathon.

I started a sad, malformed jog. My legs hated me for what I was doing, and I hated them right back. With every step, I could feel barbs of pain in my feet. Each one was a clear sign that a blister had formed. I thought about the pleasure I would take in lancing them later, and then I whispered, "Come on. You got this," and laughed again about the cow.

A minute later though, I felt like an asshole. I thought of the friends I had on Facebook who were related to cops. Some even had the Blue Lives Matter flag in their profiles. I had always sworn off talking politics on social media, and I could already imagine the hurt feelings, the resulting debates, the people who would link to the Dr. Dre and Snoop song, the thinly veiled racist responses, the generic, party rhetoric responses, the people who would link to the Sublime song, the threats to drop me as a friend, the threats to tell their cop relatives, the threats to make me do the song the next time I was at karaoke, the dislikes, the likes, the smiling emojis, the angry emojis, the emojis that made no sense, and the string of cow memes.

I needed to do something. I could delete the post altogether, or just add a note underneath—something to explain it was just a joke or that your brain goes to strange places when mid-marathon.

But then I hit that hill, and none of it mattered anymore.

Joel Worford

The Naked Eye

For as much as Jeremiah disliked middle school, he hated Sunday school even more. The twenty-minute drive from the suburbs into downtown along with the church's menacing, castle-like exterior, dirty-carpeted floors, and mothy-smelling old people were enough to turn off any thirteen-year-old. To make matters worse, all Jeremiah's school friends went to Woodstone United Methodist, a small church in the suburbs, where they played Christian rock and talked about how much Jesus loves everybody. Woodstone was walking distance from Jeremiah's house and he couldn't understand why his parents insisted that he needed to spend time with "his people" every Sunday. His friends in the suburbs were his people. Still, he knew what his mother meant. When the appeal to proximity fell through, Jeremiah turned to the academic. He begged his mother, Miranda, to let him study his Bible Sunday morning, in place of making the commute into the heart of Lynchburg's ghetto.

"It will help me practice my reading," Jeremiah insisted, knowing that this was his only real shot. Jeremiah could already read on an eleventh-grade level, an impressive feat in the eyes of college admissions boards and a convenient way to make everyone hate you in a society of seventh graders.

"You need the community," his mother replied. Her eyes drooped, having had this argument so many times, but her resolve remained unwavering.

Jeremiah fought his hardest in these disputes, puffing up his five-foot frame, waving his long, thin arms, and using all of the resources available in his eleventh-grade-level brain to make a strong counterargument.

"But it's so long, it's cutting into my study time for Monday."

"But the pastor doesn't talk about things that matter to me."

"But the other kids say bad words and are bad influences on me."

"But God said I should learn on my own."

Miranda responded by signing Jeremiah up for the youth choir. Once a week, the two piled into Miranda's old beat-up red Maxima and Jeremiah waved goodbye to his big blue house. He looked at the forest surrounding their cul-de-sac, and the neighboring homes spaced comfortably apart. Jeremiah stared up at the towering trees framing a clear blue sky, knowing this view would soon be replaced by the abandoned businesses and weed-covered buildings of downtown Lynchburg.

•••

The first few weeks, upon arrival at the church, Jeremiah's mother locked the car doors for her and Jeremiah to sit in the Maxima on the narrow city street in front of the church and wait until the first person showed up (thirty minutes late) to unlock the doors of the church so rehearsal (more like practice) could begin.

"That's what you call 'CP time,'" Miranda said, in response to Jeremiah's complaints. The first time she said this, Jeremiah looked at her in confusion.

"You know what that is?" his mother asked.

Jeremiah shook his head "no."

Miranda responded, "That stands for colored people time. Black folks is always late."

Jeremiah noticed how whenever his mother said things black people should say she said them the way black people should say them. Jeremiah didn't know what this meant, but his mother always smiled when he pointed it out.

The first rehearsal on a Tuesday in March didn't go so smoothly and Jeremiah hoped the fallout after the mishap would be enough to help him see his way out. Things got messy after two of the older kids, Juwan and Darrell, started picking on a girl named Sydney, telling her that her "pussy smelled like fish."

"Oh shit, he tryin'a wet." Jeremiah watched and listened as Darrell egged his friend on. Juwan stood next to Sydney with his chest puffed out like Popeye, post-spinach consumption. Sydney's chest, modestly sized for a sixteen-year-old, stuck out to meet Juwan's, almost touching the long silver chain draped around his thick, veiny neck as she retaliated with her own smack.

"Boy, run off tuh yo grandmamma and ask where yo daddy is." Sydney turned away with a hand flip that Jeremiah thought made her look like the new Queen of England come straight out of Bebe's kids. All of the kids responded with "oohs" while the choir director, Ms. Lucinda, moved in to catch Juwan's arm before he could strike back.

"Y'all cut out this foolishness," Ms. Lucinda yelled. She continued to berate the instigators for a few minutes that felt like a few hours to Jeremiah. The room went silent, except for the creaking of clergy member's feet on the old red-carpeted steps outside the sanctuary. Jeremiah looked up at the chandelier, which gave the room its only bit of light save for the little amount that penetrated the church's multicolored stained glass windows. Jeremiah could've sworn during the silence that the room got darker. He looked down at his toes and ran his fingers through his short curly hair while Ms. Lucinda continued to tear into the other kids. Much to Jeremiah's relief, she never once looked at him.

After Ms. Lucinda finished, the group tried to move on with practice. Jeremiah noticed how the parents of the kids involved sat real quiet and wore that same tired, worried look his mother sometimes wore. He noticed their tired was a more exhausted tired and their worry was a more desperate worry than his mother's worry. Rehearsal ended about two hours early that night.

On the way home, Jeremiah was sure that he'd be out for good. Instead, his mother affirmed that they would be back the next week. Jeremiah stared in disbelief.

"But Mom, can you believe what Juwan said? That was disgusting!" Jeremiah pleaded, his voice rising in pitch. He waved his hands in the air while he talked as if trying to conduct his argument like a symphony orchestra. Jeremiah's mother kept calm, as she always did when he got excited, holding the steering wheel with both hands without letting her eyes leave the road.

"Those boys need Jesus," she replied. She paused before concluding, "And so do you." Jeremiah's mom reached down and turned up the radio to hear the new James Fortune single.

And so that was it. Jeremiah resolved that there was nothing he could do. That night, he stared out the car window at the green hills that sloped down to meet the highway and the sky, which split into sections of orange, navy blue, and black. Jeremiah thought about school the next day, where he would be around people he could relate to again. He decided that if choir practice was just once a week, he could endure, so long as he would get to see his friends the next day and forget about the kids from downtown.

•••

At school the day after the first choir rehearsal, Jeremiah sat with his usual group of friends, Adrian, John, and Logan. Jeremiah liked sitting with them because they also enjoyed making up card games and coming up with new ideas for action figures and anime drawings. Jeremiah knew Logan from elementary school and met John through a seventh-grade computer science class where the two of them practically instructed the teacher. When Adrian transferred in from a private school on the other side of town, Jeremiah saw him standing alone in the gym with his Dragon Ball Z T-shirt on and decided he would make a good addition to their friend group. Three months later and the four were inseparable, joined at the altar of nerdiness.

"So how was the ghetto last night?" Adrian asked with a smile. The four friends moved down the school hallway between the red and black lockers that sat a few feet beneath a low ceiling. The hall was bright and crowded. The group walked almost in unison, four skinny bodies marching through a sea of averted stares, broken up by the occasional side-glance.

Logan turned towards Jeremiah after hearing Adrian's question. "Yeah, are you okay? I don't see any bullet wounds." Logan's voice rose into a laugh as he finished.

John remained silent and watched without saying anything. Jeremiah smiled in response to his friend's prodding.

"No, but I did see a fight." Jeremiah's excitement was evident in relating the news. He told his friends all about the crazy things that kids from "the ghetto" say and do. The others listened, looking on with animated expressions as if they were hearing a first-person account of their favorite childhood fairy tale. Jeremiah, feeling as if he gained some new credibility by having ventured into what his friends called "the hood," smiled at their every reaction.

"What the heck does it mean to 'wet'?" Adrian asked.

"Sounds dirty," Logan smirked. John laughed and Adrian smiled in return.

"Yeah, beats me," Jeremiah replied. He paused before continuing. "But thank God people around here aren't saying it."

•••

The next week at choir rehearsal Jeremiah had his first real interaction with one of the kids at his church. The boy's name was Keith, a short chubby kid with a small Afro and light skin. When all the kids were asked to clap on time, someone kept missing the two and four.

Keith pointed at Jeremiah. "It's him!"

Ms. Lucinda turned on Keith. Jeremiah knew she would come to his defense since Ms. Lucinda often called him her "breath of fresh air" that helped her "keep her sanity" during these rehearsals. She placed her hand on her hip as she addressed Keith. "Boy, what makes you think that it's him for?"

Keith kept his finger pointed at Jeremiah. "Cause he white, ain't got no rhythm."

The other kids busted out laughing. Jeremiah stared at Keith blankly, sure that his comment was not meant as a compliment, yet trying to find a way to take it as a friendly joke.

Ms. Lucinda scowled at Keith. "He as black as you."

Keith looked at Jeremiah and shook his head. Jeremiah saw the look on Keith's face and wished it would change. He wished Keith would look at him the same way he looked at Juwan and the other kids. The look Jeremiah got instead was very different. It was the kind of look his mother would give the television when she saw that some teenager downtown had gotten killed "fighting over a little girl." She would shake her head and reaffirm that "those kids need Jesus," before changing the channel.

On the way to the car, Jeremiah saw his mother talking quietly to Ms. Lucinda. He imagined Keith wouldn't bother him again, but wondered if not being bothered was really what he wanted. Jeremiah thought about how confidently the kids downtown talked and acted around each other and wondered why he was so different. After all, they were "his people," as his mother said. Yet still, Jeremiah didn't feel comfortable around them. There was something about the way they talked, the way they acted, that Jeremiah couldn't connect with. There was a lack of self-consciousness and boldness to it; they lived as if no higher authority existed that could touch them. Jeremiah never felt such invincibility—his mother always reminded him of all the things he had and how easily the simplest mistakes in life could take them away. Jeremiah thought of the look of admiration on his friend's face when he talked about "the ghetto." He remembered the look on Keith's face when he called him "white." Jeremiah tried to refocus on seeing his friends the next day but couldn't escape this new feeling of dissonance.

•••

The next day, in a dimly lit History classroom, Jeremiah sat at a rectangular table with his three best friends, engaged in another debate over how to plan the weekend's adventures.

"I'm telling you guys, we should do a Harry Potter marathon." Jeremiah waved his index finger at Adrian and smiled as he talked. "It would be intense. Can you imagine if we could make it through all six movies? Come on, let's try it."

The group resisted against Jeremiah, insisting instead on watching the new episode of *Tosh.0,* something that they could at least talk about in class without being met with eye rolls and not-so-subtle whispers from their classmates.

"But come on," Jeremiah continued, smiling as he made one last plea. "The new one is coming out Friday. We've gotta watch all the ones leading to it."

Logan shook his head and smirked. "God, you're so white, Jeremiah," he said as he pushed his wide-framed glasses up his nose.

Adrian laughed as a few of the other kids in class turned their heads and grinned. John gave a brief chuckle towards Logan, who gave a nod of approval in return and then turned back to his desk.

Jeremiah gave an enthusiastic smile to let everyone know that he was okay with Logan's comment. He knew this was what was expected of him since Logan wasn't a racist. He and Jeremiah were friends after all. Still, Jeremiah couldn't help remembering Keith's same comment from the night before. There wasn't the same disgust in Logan's tone that Keith had, but there was still a judgment there, as if Jeremiah fell short of some standard and, as a result, he was "white." The idea made Jeremiah feel the same uneasiness as from the night before. He turned his head towards the front of the classroom, still faking a smile when the teacher began.

•••

Jeremiah had a new strategy for the next week's choir rehearsal. He decided he needed to prove that he could fit in as well with "his people" as with his friends from the suburbs. After all, why else would his mother insist so much upon him spending time around other black people unless that was what she wanted? When Ms. Lucinda asked him if he wanted a solo part, he responded the way he thought one of the other kids might respond.

"Shit, I ain't no singer," Jeremiah said, placing his hands on his back and reclining lazily. Without looking at Ms. Lucinda, Jeremiah continued, "Let somebody else do that shit."

Jeremiah saw the choir director's puzzled look and felt a stab of remorse. A few of the other kids looked at each other with raised eyebrows. A couple girls laughed in the corner, but otherwise, everybody kept quiet.

Ms. Lucinda looked at him sideways. "Alright," she replied with a warning tone, before moving on to offer the next candidate the part. Jeremiah looked back to see his mother in the back of the church, watching with a look that he'd never seen on her face before. Jeremiah knew she wouldn't be happy about this.

"Don't you ever talk to one of the older folk like that again," Miranda said on the way out of the church, walking fast toward the narrow street without looking at Jeremiah. "You hear me, boy?" she asked as she yanked the car door open.

"Yes," Jeremiah replied, avoiding Miranda's eyes. Frightened by his mother's silence, Jeremiah spent the ride home looking up at the stars and wondering which ones were planets. He envied the fact that the naked eye, or at least an uneducated one, couldn't discern them. Jeremiah wasn't sure if it was his inability to see or their inability to be seen that prevented him from making the distinction, but either way, he coveted such invisibility.

•••

Jeremiah thought that maybe his friends at school would react differently to his new swagger. Since they admired his stories about the kids downtown so much, Jeremiah figured his new "blackness" would gain him a higher level of respect. Jeremiah decided to give it a shot during gym class. Puffing out his chest like he'd seen Juwan do at choir rehearsal, Jeremiah strutted over to Adrian, who stood getting ready to serve a volleyball to John.

"Yo man, I'm tired of this volleyball shit," Jeremiah knocked the ball out of Adrian's hand. "That shit is gay as fuck."

Logan walked over from across the net and gave Jeremiah a bemused look. "Why are you talking like that?"

Jeremiah shifted his feet uncomfortably. He suddenly felt his arms hanging awkwardly by his side. "Talking like what?"

"Um, like real black people actually talk," Logan said, rolling his eyes.

"I don't know what you mean, I always talk like this." Jeremiah responded, bending his long arms at the waist, palms facing the gym ceiling rafters.

Logan laughed. "Okay, Kanye."

"Whatever, man," Jeremiah replied. He stared down at his oversized light blue jeans hanging over torn Nike sneakers. He suddenly felt very aware of his small arms and short height compared to his three friends.

"Just accept it, Jeremiah, you're one of us," Adrian said, putting his arm around Jeremiah's shoulder. John nodded his head.

•••

When lunchtime came around, the cafeteria was full and noisy. The smell of pizza and stale potatoes permeated the air. Jeremiah listened as Logan gave his usual rant on how Barack Obama's policies would surely lead to the catastrophic end of America as we know it. Jeremiah noticed that, as usual, it didn't take long for Logan to turn to the philosophical.

"You see, Jeremiah, there's a difference between black people and niggers." Logan waved his defined, thin arms as he spoke, wearing a half grin. His eyes were sharp beneath a pair of black-framed fake glasses. Jeremiah saw Adrian and John glance uncertainly at him before laughing to assure Jeremiah that what Logan said was a joke.

Logan continued, "See Jeremiah, you're a black person like, you're cool, but those kids downtown that hang on the corners, those are niggers. It's not that hard, if you're a good person, you're black, and if you're a sack of shit, then you're a nigger."

Jeremiah smiled and forced a laugh. He was happy to finally be acknowledged as a black person, but couldn't help feeling that most black people didn't have to tolerate the way Logan talked. Jeremiah understood that Logan would never talk like this around the kids downtown, yet around Jeremiah it was okay because he was "white." Hoping his acceptance of Logan's theory would end the discussion on it, Jeremiah kept smiling. At seeing Jeremiah's smile, Logan, Adrian, and John all laughed even harder. This cycle carried on with Logan explaining how Morgan Freeman, Rihanna, and Beyoncé were black people, while Kanye West, O.J. Simpson, and almost any rapper constituted a "nigger."

After the laughter died down, Logan's eyes narrowed and he turned towards Adrian and John before giving Jeremiah a mistrustful glance.

"That Obama though...he's a nigger." Logan took a long sip out of his chocolate milk carton as Adrian and John broke into raucous laughter. Jeremiah joined in, hoping that if he laughed hard enough, he would find Logan's comments funny as well.

•••

The fourth week of choir rehearsal, all of the kids sat outside, waiting for Ms. Lucinda to come unlock the doors. Juwan, Keith, and a group of other kids from the neighborhood stood beside the street, clustered tight together. A cop car sat parked in front of a dirty white house across from the church. Jeremiah sat on the hard, concrete steps leading up to the church doors, away from the other kids, resting his head on his ashy knees, which he hugged tight to his chest. He'd given up on fitting in and decided to take comfort in the solitude of his own thoughts. Miranda told him she would be right back from the gas station, so until then, he decided he would disappear.

Jeremiah looked up at the blue and yellow evening sky, trying to identify the clouds as animals. He looked down to notice Juwan and the other kids staring at him.

"Hey, yo, Jeremiah. Come here, man." Juwan waved his hand, beckoning Jeremiah to the edge of the street. Jeremiah noticed the change in Juwan's tone. None of the kids from church had ever spoken to him as if he were a part of the group before.

Jeremiah jumped up and rushed down the church steps to where the other kids stood. "What's up?" he asked, facing Juwan.

Juwan pointed his chubby finger towards the cop car, his eyelids drooping over a sly grin. "Hey man, we wanna make you a bet."

Jeremiah followed Juwan's finger and hesitated before responding. "What's that?" he asked.

Juwan kept his finger pointed at the cop car as he continued. "We was gon' scratch the paint off that cop car, man." Juwan pulled a knife out of his pocket and extended it towards Jeremiah. "We was figuring, with the way you talked to Ms. Lucinda last week, you'd be wantin' to help. That was some bold-ass shit, man. I respect that."

"Thanks," Jeremiah muttered. He looked at the cop car and then looked at the street corner that his mom would be coming around any minute. Jeremiah remembered the look on her face when he talked back to Ms. Lucinda. He remembered his friend's indifference and mockery of his feigned "blackness."

The other kids looked at Jeremiah and Juwan expectantly. Juwan held the knife out to Jeremiah with a slight smile, his eyes brimming with curiosity. Jeremiah looked down at the knife in Juwan's hand and held up his own in rejection. "No thanks," he replied.

Juwan dropped the knife by his side and grinned. "Damn," he said.

Keith stepped up from behind him. "Man, I told you he was a bitch-ass little white nigga." He grabbed the knife from Juwan's hand and pointed it at Jeremiah. "How about I say 'do it, or I'll beat yo ass'?"

Jeremiah took a step back and tripped, landing on a grassy slope behind the concrete sidewalk. Keith towered over him and laughed. All the other kids joined in except Sydney, who stepped in front of Keith, standing inches away from his face.

"Nigga, I don't see you doing shit." Sydney said, her short, jet-black hair shaking. She moved her neck while talking; her heels and long legs almost put her at Keith's height. She pointed down at Jeremiah. "At least this nigga got some sense."

Keith's brown cheeks turned red. He took a step back and pointed Juwan's knife at the cop car. "You wanna see some shit? Bitch, I'll do shit."

Keith crossed the street and began slashing at the tires on the car. Jeremiah knew what would happen before it happened. While Keith stood there making little progress on destroying the cop car, an officer appeared out of the house directly in front of Keith. It was as if he'd never stopped watching the church kids, waiting for them to make him do his job.

"Oh shit!" Juwan yelled, his grin giving way to a scowl. He ran up the street, away from the officer, as the rest of the group dispersed. At that moment, Jeremiah's mom pulled up next to the curb. Jeremiah remained lying on the grassy hill in front of the church. The officer, wearing black and gold, pressed Keith facedown on the cop car as he talked into his portable radio.

Jeremiah's mother closed the car door violently and rushed up the sidewalk. Her face contorted into a grimace as she knelt down to Jeremiah. "What on earth happened here?" she asked.

Jeremiah stumbled onto his feet and fell into his mother's embrace, arms hanging limply by his side. The officer across the street pushed Keith into his car. He looked at Jeremiah and Miranda, surveyed them for a second, and then got into his vehicle and drove off.

"I didn't do anything, Mom." Jeremiah mumbled into his mother's stomach.

Miranda took Jeremiah's hand and led him to the car. They drove back home without the radio on. Jeremiah told his mom what happened as she watched the road with her lip turned upwards.

"Those kids need Jesus," she said.

•••

At school the next day, Jeremiah heard a few kids talking about the arrest downtown, but not many knew it happened right outside of Jeremiah's church. It took Jeremiah's friends until the afternoon buses were coming to make the connection between the school gossip and Jeremiah's church, located on the same street as the incident. They confronted Jeremiah about it while standing in the school's common area among clusters of students scattered about the room, some standing in the middle of the floor, others leaning against the wall. The three stood in their usual corner next to a window overlooking a large green field.

"It was your church?" Adrian wore a look of astonishment as Jeremiah confirmed that he had watched the events take place. Adrian stared with his mouth open and excitement in his eyes.

"What did you do?" Adrian asked.

Jeremiah shrugged. "Nothing really, I just saw it happen," he said.

Adrian gave John and Logan a wide-eyed look as he laughed. "Man, you could've been arrested!" he said.

"Yeah, I guess so." Jeremiah replied, smiling weakly.

Logan looked straight ahead without smiling. He finally turned towards Jeremiah. Jeremiah noticed Logan's eyes staring through his glasses, hard and intense. He was clearly trying to work through his thoughts on the situation. His silence almost betrayed a sort of envy that Jeremiah could see but couldn't quite comprehend. Suddenly breaking out of his trance, Logan looked at Jeremiah.

"See," he said, smirking. "You and that kid that got caught, it just shows you the difference. Niggers and black people."

Adrian laughed and John nodded his head. Jeremiah paused, looking out the window at the green tree-covered mountains reaching into a cloudless sky. He wondered if accepting Juwan's offer to take the knife and then getting arrested would've made him a "black person" or a "nigger." He couldn't decide if he was supposed to act the way his mom taught him to act and get mocked or if he should act the way "his people" were expected to act and be celebrated, but fall the way his people were expected to fall. Jeremiah looked at Logan, who was still laughing, eyes shut tight beneath his plastic glasses. Adrian and John continued to laugh as well. Jeremiah forced a smile and joined in.

Poetry

"Arches by the Sea," photography by Ramsey Mathews

Mary Jo Balistreri

How Light Casts Its Net

Remember the orange summer of flowers, gardens
that opened onto chrysanthemums as we sauntered
along the avenue, iced-mochas in hand, looking for bargains
the rush of autumn left behind?

Remember the black sleeveless dress you bought that day
marked down to a ridiculously low price? The way you twirled
in the full skirt, black sash tied in front?
As light as a breeze you said.

And now a breathless day in October, sun burning
on your bare arms, you stand in another kind of garden,
hem of your black dress barely moving.
The white heat intensifies. Steeple bells peal the hour.

The priest empties your husband's cremains, scatters them
like a path in the rich, dark soil. You look down,
shards of bone too bright in the glare. Your hand plucks
at the skirt's cotton fabric. It clings to your skin in the heat.

Nina Bennett

The Indifference of Rain

Rain, and I'm on Main Street again,
searching for a parking space
on a one-way street in a college town.

"Rainy Days and Mondays" on the car radio
reminds me of Karen Carpenter,
makes me think of Pammy. It was raining
the day we found her, the day we pounded
on her apartment door and windows,
bellowed her name in two-part harmony.
Upstairs neighbor said he hadn't seen her
for a few days, told us to call the cops.

My friend and I waited on the sidewalk
while raindrops pinged off metal garbage cans
like BBs our younger brothers fired at stop signs
on steamy July nights.

Roy Bentley

Show Me the Face of My Great-Grandfather before He Burned

Take back the afternoon light at Neon Junction in Letcher County,
the crying of my father in infancy on the porch in a basket of sheets.
Take back the stories of Quiller Bentley, my great-grandfather, setting
ablaze the underbrush growing over his field rather than labor to clear it.
Take back rogue gusts turning flames in his direction and then the flames
encircling him in retreat. Take back a narcotic blur of screams and a body
in rebellion throughout one night and a day and then another night. Leave
me his bland face before all this and I will give you back the ruby skin of
lesser burned places, his failing to account for an insurgency in the wind.

We are, after all, the sum of our mistakes as well as answering for them.
I forfeit wanting an answer for swindles after palm-to-palm handshakes,
the whole of the history of the first Kentuckians and the theft-by-contact
and ages of poverty at the hands of armies of robber barons. I'll forego
remembrance of joy at seeing my Grandmother Bentley's face brighten
at any suggestion of leaving Neon Junction—not the thing but an echo
of the thing, not sorrow or crying out after sorrow but one man raising
himself to curse God and fall back onto cool sheets turned and turning
midnight black and pomegranate red, the colors of his difficult dying.

George Bishop

Cards

Ever since I quit drinking, the shuffle
never seems to end. So, I'm sitting
between addictions trying to remember
my last hand. I can clearly see an ace
although the suit's worn like the date

on a rare coin. I always kept a seven
of something somewhere secret because
secrets were all that really mattered.
It's been a long life of gambling myself
away. However, the game might be

changing. My shadow's got the deal
and I sort of trust his hands, the way
they shift the darkness like a barmaid
mixing her best story and smile into
an endless last call only I can hear.

George Bishop

Home

I still have the key to the house where
I never lived, the rough brass buffed
pearl-like by the inside of an old man's

pocket who walked too far to get back.
But, let's say he does, doesn't feel a need
to knock, isn't here to look for answers,

already knows the other side of nothing.
It's how I fall asleep most nights now,
standing there, still as the shape of a lock.

Rose Mary Boehm

Half remembered

In the cornucopia of my life
none of the pain remains.
The scabs have healed
and disappeared.
That's proof enough.
But I cannot recall a single hurt.
The knife that cut deep,
a film before my eyes.
Yet the years erased the ache,
except for that soft pressure of your hand
just where my neck and shoulders meet
"steering" me along the Rue du Bac.

G. F. Boyer

All My Smoky Aunts

I'd slink along the blossom-papered
kitchen walls and eye those toucans—
my smoky aunts—flitting around
their sister, my mother, the brown-
feathered common junco.

My mother bustled and fussed,
emptying ashtrays, cranking the windows
all the way out.

My aunts' Camel smoke sashayed up—
exotic, lacy, blue—while I ate
corn chowder with a wooden spoon,
enthralled by their cigarettes,
their wheat-sack lizard bird-leg skin,
their husky laughter,
their meanness and sin.

G. F. Boyer

The Virgin Queen

     She leaves, trailed by drones
who vie to be the chosen one:
to win, to die.

     Like some Kama Sutra feat,
the queen and drone meet and merge mid-air,

       forward, backward,
       upside down,
       at two hundred feet.

Stolid worker bees get back to work on their
obsessive math,

constructing hexagons of wax,
carrying water, hauling pollen baskets on their shins,

       stuffed satchels fringed
       with blossom dust.

And a plum tree's sweating globes grow fat

       and fall, to burst with sugar
near the spent drone's withered shell.

Alan Catlin

Wilde as the Clown Prince of Londontown

> "Yes, I always call by their Christian names people whom I like.
> People I dislike I call something else."
> —Oscar Wilde, *The Trials of Oscar Wilde*

Punch would have him drawn as an unseemly
giant, protruding from the docks,
hair brushed aside from his forehead,
parted dead center, a hydrocephalic in jesters'
cap and bells, suit of the clown Touchstone
to Queensbury's Lear, trumpeting his proclamation
that Oscar was an "Unnatural sodomite."
Not even the importance of being Oscar can
save him from being reviled, made naked
as the most commonest of men caricatured
in the language of the gutter no one can
refute. Exiled, after the disgrace, after Reading
Jail, after writing the magnificent *De Profundis,*
now penniless Oscar drinks champagne against
the Doctor's orders, retiring to his death bed
where the last image in this world is that of
the hovering, officious hotelier, waiting with
a servile smile to remove the gold-plated dentures
immediately after his death,
as sure recompense for the room.

Joan Colby

The River's Edge

The river boils below the dam.
Froth like a frosted wedding cake.
You'd drown in that vortex,
Pulled down and down by the trolls
Who abide beneath bridges.
Those old tales hold truths
Like a curative herb, foxglove
To strengthen the heart, honey to soothe
A wound, the milk of the poppy
Loading pain in the holds
Of the ships that sail the moon.
Philosophers seek the stone
That weighs on the mind, the mother-of-pearl
That lines the compact made with love.
You say once we had time or thought
We did. Years to cherish, to decide,
To abandon or seize. Now
A sign says this road ends
And yes. Yes it does.

Joan Colby

Black Moon

Turns away like a modest woman.
Burkha-clad.
Nun.
Sorceress.
A night for spells
For the owl and the hunted.

Look up, a slit of light
Where a pregnant woman cradles her belly,
How she holds the indistinguishable
Curve of reflection
On this last day of September.
The virgins flee into the calendar
As if refusals bestow sanctity.

Squint to acknowledge the moon
In her shriven phase
As she addresses the ignorance
Of those who claim to see
Nothing. The doubters
Who trust only their five senses.

William Doreski

Body Men

At the body shop, a mist of paint engrains the air and coats our lungs with luxury colors. We could live here in a fossil state too thick for the world to penetrate. By engorging on rusted sheet metal, we could toughen ourselves tougher than legal documents. Wrecked cars slump in the yard. Their sculptural demise ennobles them. The deaths they've enclosed anoint them with an aura of vengeance. The two body men are deep in their seventies. Warping metal to flatter the aerodynamics of the contemporary mind has kept them young and nimble. They vault over the roofs and hoods of cars without scraping the paint. They caress fenders and doors to smooth them into submission. We watch with envy boiling over. If only we possessed such a sense of touch. If only our colors meshed the way their touch-ups do. What would it cost to enhance ourselves with factory-approved replacement organs? What would it cost to streamline ourselves to speed through the rest of our days screaming with flame and blue exhaust? Dents and dings, scrapes and crumples. The body men look turgid as old-fashioned novelists, but they approach their work with style too daring for *Vogue* and a tenderness that's nothing but mercy. If we lie at their feet they might stoop to embrace us, and then all four of us would join a choir that would ascend, singing, into some trademarked shade of blue.

Karen George

Night Canyon

*—Found poem composed/modified from words
of Georgia O'Keeffe's painting titles*

A ladder left against a cliff
Near its rim, a lake clouded purple

a drawn green door
twelve plum-black crows

rise out of Jimsonweeds
toward blue stars

Beth Gordon

Watching Woody Allen Movies on Memorial Day Weekend

After you mowed the yard and I swept the deck, dusted the piano, poured blue gel into
both toilet bowls, after we over-ate at an Asian restaurant in a nearby college town,
argued feebly over who would pay the bill, drove past familiar man-made lakes and
corporate farms, after the dogs chastised us, ignored our insistence on completing
chores and slept without dreams in the sunshine, after we drank two Bloody Mary's
each, after you asked for more hot sauce and horseradish, after you told me about your
favorite day in Ireland, your walk to the lighthouse with apples and cheese in your
pockets, after we watched large raindrops, danced to distant thunder, after we talked
about the pros and cons of romantic love, the rehabilitation of injured rats, the way
we both refused to snort cocaine, we sat in chairs, we watched Woody Allen movies
until we questioned our creative intent, until we longed for bleakness and neurotic
dachshunds, until we imagined our unwritten childhoods living below an active roller
coaster, until we asked if we had ever been as young and wide-eyed as Diane Keaton in
Annie Hall, until we consulted tarot cards and old maps, until we fell in love with New
York City, because we can't fall in love with each other.

D. A. Gray

Jazz

Forget what they taught you
in science class. The L word is a sound
pushed up and out from the gut.

Maybe it's the silence that makes two,
staring across a dusky blue room, hear
the note. Something from the past
is trying its hardest to get out.

The trick is not to choke. Sometimes
the body grows fearful and constricts,
somewhere in the throat.

Once I tried to play piano and the notes,
though correct, lived separate lives in the air,
one falling loosely behind another.

Then, I thought the spaces were just that—emptiness,
free of tree-branch moans, tire-to-asphalt wails,
percussive brown rivers, and the throbbing
bass of civilizations, each passing through
the silent self.
              When we met, each body began to flow
through a rainy street, improvising like jazz;
vibrations lingered and we, unsure where one note
ended, where another one began, suddenly unafraid.

Hayley Mitchell Haugen

Grimm Girl, fresh from the forest, gets lost

without her breadcrumbs leading the one way home.
So many crosswalks, shopping malls, exits
and entrances with their slick-tiled floors and chandeliers,
but still, she thinks she can make it here, beyond
the gingerbread cupboards and wishing wells.

She burns her yellow knee patches, wears white silk
in the mornings and winter gabardine. She gets credit
for now, and a boyfriend on Main, and lets her house
go dirty.

There's so many ways to get paid for a living,
she can wait it out awhile. Just as easy to sleep,
she says, finally, without the cock crowing, the evil light
of the twelve o'clock moon, and that damned red devil
behind her lace-ups, keeping her moving along.

Hayley Mitchell Haugen

Inside L O V E

(for David)

On the outskirts of campus
on a weedy patch of neglected grass,
the cement L leans heavily
towards traffic on 7th Street.
Half the size of local eucalyptus,
it looks like a student project
not quite begun, in need
of a fresh white coat to paint
over spring break graffiti. The O
is no great feat of engineering,
rolling, it seems, in a slow-motion
lopsided dance past student parking.
The V spreads wide in a sign of peace,
a testament to the era that bred it,
and the E, it simply faces east,
pigeons nesting in its elbows.
So this is *love*—weather-beaten
and shat upon, limbs so akimbo
anyone could miss it. On odd days
an old man comes and plays
his shiny trumpet—resting his back
somewhere up against L through E,
where the acoustics do their best for him.
Would it surprise you to know
that I stop and listen then?
That the traffic becomes a dull hum.
My books, my papers, my complaints
all fall away. And I think of you,
your image rising inside my mind,
like the single sweetest note
from inside love.

Dianna Henning

Rhubarb Season

The rooster crowed at the first

strike of light, awaking the stone child who
held her own child, and was

herself a child. In England, the first

rhubarb of the year is harvested
by candlelight to enhance a more
tender, sweeter stalk. There's even

a *Rhubarb Triangle,* where growing-sheds
dot the land. This resembles wonder. Salt

on rhubarb is what you remember. You
offer a bite to the stone child. She
wrinkles her face into a smile. You'll never

get used to the way memory
makes you live many lives. In a single season
of rhubarb,

countless stone children are unearthed.

Dianna Henning

The Village Lives in the Sheep; the Sheep in the Village

Several, ancient and steadfast,
lounge on the green hills, while others,

braver, escape stone walls
to wander as though touring the nearby; shags

of wool hanging off their chests, their eyes
electric with storms. Those

are the ones that return
each century, stalwart and fat—their gait

an old man's gait or the limping
gait of the man who runs

Ambleside's butcher shop, his apron
blood-stiff, a cleaver in hand. Some

villagers think of sheep as apostles,
especially those that dare stray,

and who, upon return to their flock
relay what they foraged;

a keening for their tribe.

Sarah Henry

Deus Ex Machina

Theoretically everything is possible
except the ending of the opera
where characters fall down dead,
then rise to sing the final aria.

Everything is possible
except the ending of the novel
you just finished and
impatiently flung aside.

Everything except the talking
heads scene in the movie
where the location
shifts to another country.

Airplanes fly to the rescue.
Ships pick up stranded children.
The swashbuckling hero
leaps from the roof.

To our dull surprise,
he makes a steady
landing, as we should
have known by now.

Mike James

The Mime

His mother never quit talking. She couldn't sew a button or not burn toast or properly use a tissue on any tear, but she could talk. No telegraph silences. Just an electric hum, long as day.

So he wanted a quiet place. He found a box, with invisible walls. Crawled right in.

After a while, after silence became as empty as a shell and the sound of his breathing was the last thing he wanted to hear, he ran his palms along the walls, hoped and hoped for the exit that was there.

Mike James

Wish Factory

Start out making a ham sandwich, end up trying to lick your elbow. Start out trying to lick your elbow, end up painting your nails. Start out painting your nails, end up in a large bubble bath with a stranger. Start out bathing joyfully with a stranger, end up making excuses for Christmas dinner. Start out making excuses for Christmas dinner, end up decorating the tree with hate notes and other handmade ornaments from throughout the year.

Seth Jani

Clear Forms

I have no understanding of radiance,
Of light's mechanics.

I know no constellations,
And even embers evade me.

But the shine, and it is
A Shine, that enters

The body during sleep,
That percolates dreams

And glistens eyes,
Leaves me wondering

Night after night,
Leaves me filling

The margins of the book.
Those lucid animals

We call illusion, those flowers
Too red to be red,

Do they leave behind hard crystals?
Flaming bits of ore?

Do their marvelous forms
Ever wake with us

In a rush of snow?

Seth Jani

Coming and Going

All day answers are falling
From the wind-napped petals
Onto the starch-colored stone.
We can stop the masquerade right here,
In the instant of summer's transition,
In the moment the page blows over
Revealing sigils of whitened moss.
We were wrong to believe
We were ever someone.
Seasons and millennia equally span
The space between us.
It doesn't matter.
We wake when we wake
And may never know
The number of our wakings.
The pear tree stoops
Its perfect umber into the yard
For the umpteenth time,
And no one ever mentions
The generations of fruit
On the valley floor.

Seth Jani

Fields

Loss was always part
Of the horizon.
It made your hands glow
With morning light,
Made you understand
The delicacy of each maneuver
Whenever you startled a swallow
From its nest.
The dream of consciousness
Cracks over the field like an egg,
Like someone's revelation of longing.
We don't return from those dark rooms
Unaltered.
They precipitate in our hearts
And the geology changes.
The older that I get
The more I am convinced
An ultimate goodness
Gives us our pain.
It wants to make us raw
That we may feel the wind
Drop its blessings.
It wants to hold us
In our mineral bodies.
It doesn't care whatever narratives
Keep us from our joy.

Seth Jani

The Balloons

Beautiful crosswork filling
The morning sky,
And some old eruption
Dotting the landscape
With gem and basalt.
No worry if we are
Better or worse than others,
Knee-deep in dragon scales
We wander the petrified forest
Collecting geodes in our hearts.
We should treat the world
As if it were made of diamonds.
Everything quietly reflected
And afterwards, just silver glass.
A plane passes over
And we don't fear modernity.
A field reveals hidden bodies
And we don't fear the eventual process.
The wicker baskets lift
From the canyon floor,
Carrying their happy passengers
Nowhere really special.

Susan Johnson

Blue And Forever Distant

Most people don't die from homesickness
but some come close, covering a canvas
with landscapes lofty and remote, home

an idea perched on a cliff. In my great-
grandfather's version, self-portrait as mountain
cabin, a trail switch-backs until it's lost in sky.

You cross to a land that doesn't speak Norwegian
you paint it instead, blue and forever distant.
I am drawn to the painting and to what is drawn

in the painting; you want to peer through
the doorway, rest by the tidy stack of wood.
Which is why we frame art like we frame

windows. There's always something going
on inside. Yet if he were to knock on my window,
old geezer smelling of linseed in a battered

paint-splattered hat, I'd probably run. I've got
my own homesickness, thank you. My own
home on a river that empties every low tide.

Jennifer Lagier

Communion of Clumsy Sisters, Stumbling Souls

"I am hungry and you give me a dictionary to decipher."
—Anne Sexton

I think of Eve
as she takes the first bite,
wipes suggestive juice
from soft, scarlet mouth.
Did she feel the hidden worm stir,
accept her guilty burden
with knowledge-tuned eyes?

Hungry Persephone opened
a blushing pomegranate
to ingest the fateful seed.
For penance, she forfeited sunlight,
condemned half a year
among the dead
in frigid underworld.

Each coveted feast,
honest articulation,
comes at a cost.
I kneel at appetite's altar,
share my truth,
take full responsibility,
let the chips fall.

Stanley McCormick

Hospital Notes: Making Peace with a Bladder Catheter

As she comes in she says, *No worries! In nursing school,*
I mastered the handling of soft parts.

But her gentle voice grates hard
on the image of a rooster's comb splayed by a hand
in a latex glove, ripping the plastic, releasing a little jiggling tube.

You don't have to watch if it bothers you. You see, you have
an issue. Your urine's blocked. That's what the catheter's for.
It's only rhetorically a rubbery tube. Think jello.

But I say, Hello,
have you ever had your glans swabbed in iodine?

Don't be funny. Let's just
jelly up. You won't feel a thing till I
inflate the balloon.

And while she works,
I think of the earth's vast wastes, erosions and eruptions,
its gooey flows. Oceans excrete sheaves of sedimentary layers.
Why not the body? Like stars, we humans are fond
of our deep ejecta. We exfoliate and expectorate. We weep,
we sweat, we blow. Menstruatejaculate. And yes, go ahead
and say it: we spit and shit, we piss, we share

This very human need to urgently rid ourselves
of life's dregs. To be less to be more
immaculate. To render remorse the full, clean stream
we hurtle back into the black river of amnesia.

Wow, is your face flushed. Please spread
your legs and hold onto the bedrail. Rest assured,
I know psychology. Do you know any, too?

And I say no, but I know
the fevered peak of pain. I know it as
the ungodly silence of the forest, and I know it as
the sight of my own knifed flesh.

Finally, she says, *Here comes the plunge, lickity split.*
But it feels more like a pike, wickedly swift,
my rarest parts, gutted and gaffed like a fish.

And when it is done she leaves me knowing
that a catheterizing of the bladder
has nothing to do with pain. Or even
excreta. It has to do with a place

Innate in all living flesh—nexus of yearning and blessed
hunger—that longs to be leaving, rejoining forever
this endless swirl of blood and spent tissues—blue issue
of oceans and stars.

Michael Minassian

Some Books

Jack calls me on the telephone
to say he has mailed me a copy
of his latest book—
"Be sure to tell me
what you think," he says.

And I remember the time we came out
of a movie theater
and overheard a couple arguing
in the parking lot—catching
every third or fourth word
slicing through the harsh winter air:
"you used to…"
"she doesn't like it when you…"
"so humiliating…."

Then the sound of a slap reaches us,
and the woman drives off leaving
her husband/boyfriend/lover
shivering red-faced under the streetlight.
Jack offers him a ride and I expect
the guy to say no, but he accepts.

Later, after we drop him off,
Jack sees two of his novels are missing
from the back seat, a few shreds of paper
on the floor of the car.
"It's OK," he says,
"some books are eaten to remember,
        some are eaten to forget."

Michael Minassian

The Disappearance

I searched the newspapers
and online for some word
of you or your sudden
disappearance,
contacted your family
and friends, knocked
on strangers' doors
posted signs in shop windows
and on telephone poles,
called the television stations
and radio talk shows
but no one knew
what happened or why,
until I saw the teeth marks
you left along my body
like a fresh tattoo
that appeared overnight
with no explanation
no trace of drugs or alcohol,
only a persistent gnawing
in my chest as if you had sewn
yourself alive, inside.

Michael Minassian

The Language of Bees

Once, I walked deep inside the woods
past the open field as far as I could,
seeking the honey hives and combs,
the nectar of the forest and homes
made of wax and the pollen of the trees,
to learn at last the language of the bees.
Opening my mouth, they flew past my lips
landing on my tongue, a wet landing strip,
forming old and new sounds together
a language of wings without feathers
renaming all the parts of the world
our speech now curled and then unfurled
every word ending with the letter Z
until all my lies now taste like sweet honey.

Robert Okaji

Simplify, as in Forget

To turn off the stove
or close the refrigerator door,

such brazen attempts to win
the aging contest or blur the mirror

of clarity—you won't say
which to blame or praise

or whether intent is implicit in
action or if I should hold my breath.

What is the freezing point of love?
When you were cold, whose

belly did you curl into, whose ear
gathered your breath and returned it

warm and with the promise of bees
producing honey? Your name floats

above my outstretched hand,
and unable to grab it, I blink and turn

away. Nothing works as it should.
I exhale. You push the door shut.

Martin Ott

We Have Microwaves that Turn into Cameras

We have a story that will make us
forget the death of something dear.
We have rows of pawned spy equipment
next to wedding rings with questionable mojo.
We have Vikings who reached Greenland
and disappeared. Wait, that one's true.
We have a fever that comes from letting
a sickness take hold of the body. Everybody.
We have a river that is muddy and a river
that can be set on fire. It is all the same river.
We have a wall in our imagination. We have
a jury of fears. We have a countdown clock.
We have a collective amnesia and the person
next to us could be our enemy or lover.
We have a way with words. This is meant
as a compliment. This is likely a tragedy.
We have a device that will cook the world
if you shove it into too small a place.

Martin Ott

You Can Go to the Moon if You Want & Here's How

You can launch a weightless tourist
and torch their money like rocket fuel.
The moon might be the barrel of a sun.
You can orbit a shy admirer afraid to look
at you like you might be an eclipse.
God points down with a waning finger.
You can board the traveling
apocalypse on its way to the dark side.
The aperture danced with our moods.
You can jettison your baggage and plant
your flag without declaring ownership.
The light never closed for good.
You can remember how to soar
in a cardboard box and moonwalk with glee.
The father's a shimmering reflection of the son.
You can feel the tug of that other eye,
a forgotten twin pulling you into the night.

James Owens

Bicycle

At the first chill of the ending
summer, the not-so-young
Mennonite wife—a blue dress
and blue, stringed bonnet

and plum sweater shut to her chin—
powers past, shoulders
forward, arms stiff,
almost too zealous for

the curve, skids, but
catches balance, pedals hard
to gain speed, her cheeks
and brow the wind has

honed nearly as far beyond
rose as her sweater—
they would be smooth
and cool to a touch—

and she smiles perhaps secretly
at the earliest, ungentle
grip of the autumn
that is certainly coming.

James Owens

After Reading "Mourning and Melancholia," I Go for a Walk

1.

The evening is cool after rain.
Among the puddles that gleam
under the chain-link fence
of the dairy processing plant,
I meet a frog half the bulk of my hand
and guide him off the road, into grass,
so he can go on eating and rutting.
Men and women are beginning
a shift beside the pasteurizing vats.
Later tonight, I think around three a.m.,
a young Anishinaabe woman
might step out onto a loading dock
for a break from the sour breath
of hot milk and might hear crickets
and the aching, lovely, clacking passage
of a slow train that comes
and leaves without stopping,
far on the other side of Highway 17.

2.

Now I walk by the rich houses
that afford views above the river,
many yards with FOR SALE signs.
I move quietly, without envy.
I've only ever stolen one thing,
as far as I recall --- a book,
a worn, water-stained copy
of Marlowe's *Doctor Faustus*
when I was eighteen years old,

and I spent a fine morning reading,
in my parents' sunlit back yard,
guiltless, delighted, knowing
nothing of what would come.
Is *not knowing* what I have lost,
since I must have lost something?

3.

Before circling back to lamps
and sleep, I touch the stations
of my way through town,
the bulldozed lot where for years
a derelict house thrived like a lung
with the tholing tones of pigeons,
another house where Mrs. Gross
lived with her son while Alzheimer's
sleeked her as innocent as untrodden
earth, and the bridge where my wife
met a wolf at night, two winters ago.
He bulked real and stiff-footed
in the middle of the road and watched
her face, awaiting his chance.
It was snowing. Just beyond
the final light, more shapes
slouched hungry from the dark.
She backed away, slow, too wise
to run, and came breathing home.

Alita Pirkopf

When Leaves Are Gone

Is it what one writes
when the last yellow glimmer
leaves
one staring at outlines
of small fingered trees
reaching for the same moon
and only briefly holding on a bit
to it?

Is it what one writes
in winter
that decides
how grim or promise green
the world is to come?

Gulls, gray geese flocked
around cold park lakes—freezing,
facing, all together against winter
wind, weather, flew up then and away
in victory signs and echoed honks

and cries we felt, all marveling,
all escaping a wet blanket winter,
gray-and-white ghost sky, day,
an Earth white as rabbit.

Serena Eve Richardson

Home on Hospice

I tried to pretty the bedroom for you—
draped Nani's pearl necklace on the headboard,
cut fresh hydrangeas for the wilted air,
and did my best to keep it cool. I read
the provided literature, knew what
to expect, let my thumb tremble and sweat,
and dripped morphine into your coma mouth.

I waited with you in your yellow room,
walls fat with decades of painting over
other hues like flush pink and mocha cream,
and watched for the creep of fingernail blue,
listened for the rattling and told you
all about how the old dogwood tree was
blooming in the still heat of the summer.

Terry Savoie

For the Paperboy Who Went Missing (September 5, 1982)

—after viewing "Who Took Johnny?"

Some say you were the first face on milk
   cartons when
      cartons were still made of waxed cardboard,
    but then we discovered you staring
back from cork bulletin boards hung in
   grocery
      stores & hardware stores or on the post
    office missing persons posters. Then
they moved you onto the Internet
   & chat rooms
      although, for us, you were forever
    frozen in that time back then, that fate-
ful morning you vanished while pulling
   your wagon
      to deliver the Sunday morning
    papers. We do admit though how well
you've kept up with the times, aging so
   artfully
      &, we might add, miraculously
    with the help of the very latest
in computer technology which
   has aged you
      before our very eyes, ten, twenty,
    even thirty marvelous years in-
to the future. Today you appear
   to us far
      easier in imaginary
    skin than any of us ever will
be in our dried up & wrinkly ones.

What we see
        before us now is not one of those
    ethereal tree-dwelling children
who forever haunt our dreams. Here you
    seem to be
        shyly emerging from the shadows
    by the side of the road, waving as
if nothing happened. Yes, you're still here
    & with us,
        taking center stage. We said it would
    happen, Johnny, knew damn well it would
        all along.

Judith Skillman

Fire Ants

You too have seen the antics,
where several surround a caterpillar,
disable and carry the inchling,
writhing into their nest.

A liquid mountain of needles
ever growing, seething as with anger
though these others
seem to follow the code of communism,

imbuing it with the palpable detachment
of true believers. Outside the anthill
no fellows lie on scraps of newspaper,
none beg for flesh or grass.

You too have wondered
whether their religion requires a sacrifice
in May, after Eliot's cruelest month
has passed, and the bears emerge.

Judith Terzi

Apple Pie

They say they want to *take the country back.*
Like a pair of shoes, hats my mother took back:
straw ones, felt ones. *Take them the hell back,*
Father would say, and we'd schlep hatboxes back
to downtown Philly. Wanamaker's had our back.
Like the Grand Canyon, Niagara Falls, back-

bone of tourism. And Yosemite, Sequoia, back-
to-back beauts. Some say, *Take the country back.*
Take it back from *Carolina snow,* hibiscus, back
from the eagle, bobcat, elk, buffalo. Haul it back
from the Joshua tree, Quercus, aspen, back
from the California drought, the humpback

with a seal on its back, shimmering bareback
of a prom dress cresting the foam, laid back
in Maui or Malibu. Oh, take Canyon de Chelly back,
red arches, reaches of the Navajo, and take back
the syllabary of Cherokee while you're at it. Back-
spin to Delancey Street: Yiddish and German, back-

to-back phonemes, Ukrainian, Italian bouncing back
and forth between pushcarts, paper boys, backs
of vaudeville seats. Take it all back. And backwards with *español,* too, right along with back-
lash. And send Guthrie's *Jesús y Rosalita* back
to the plazas of Oaxaca and Monterrey. Send back

Bartholdi's green giant to *Vive la France,* back
with brie, French fries, eau de toilette. Take back
the whole kit and caboodle and lingerie. Piggyback
the railroad and dim sum. *Come gather 'round* back,

The Times They Are A-Changin' fast track back
like the end of daylight saving. And don't back

off. Even the Walk of Fame's stars taken aback:
Sinatra's and Bogart's and Garbo's shoved back
into anonymity. And Ella's. *A-Tisket, A-Tasket* back
into her buttery chords, scatting left-right back
into the imagination of America. And out back
Brooklyn, Willy Loman lying flat on his back

waiting for a callback, straining for a comeback,
like Desire slithering back onto a streetcar or the back
of an Alabama bus humming the *Saint Louis Blues.*

Jim Zola

Reasons for Leaving

A girl in white shorts and a red-checked shirt
leans against the open door of a blue truck.
She seems to be trying to make some decision
as she rocks from foot to foot. She's too far
away, too far to tell if she's pretty,
how young, or who she is speaking to.
Give me time. By the end of this
you might know more than you want to—
the color of her panties, the reason for the scar
on her big toe, why she is standing
in this almost-empty parking lot
half in half out of a beat-up truck.
Give me time and she will become
sister, daughter, wife. Or I
will become the man in the driver's seat
sucking on a cherry cough drop.
I'm offering her a ride out of this town
where strangers know too much. Her panties
are sky blue. She dropped a butcher's knife
one drunken night and it cut clear through
her shoe. She rocks from foot to foot.
I watch her crawl in, slam the door.
Lock it. She says, Did you notice
that guy at the edge of the lot watching us?

Jim Zola

Scuppernong on the Mother Vine

It's more the way it feels on my tongue,
not the tart plum juiciness of it,
breaking through the scorched skin,
but the syllables that fuzz my senses,
make me drunk on words. Never mind
the jelly in hillbillied jars
at the farmers market, chunky sweet hell
ready for toast. Or the wine, rowdy.
Muscadine, the toughest of grapes
leaving the Carmenere and Petit Rouge
to raisin in shame. Never mind the taste
of dirt, the woody hints. I love the sound
of it. Beyond Wollongong, Chittagong,
places I will never venture.
I repeat the word, Scuppernong,
my evensong. Still my heart fails me.

Essays

"Georgia Guidestone," photography by Diane Kistner

Marc Mayer

Nothing but a Heartache

I tried to escape it. I really tried. Knowing I had a family history of heart disease, I did everything in my power to forestall any possibility of the problem. I exercised. I ran. I biked. I wasn't running marathons or posing for the front cover of *Ripped,* but I was exercising as much as I could while still holding down a job and trying to stay on a first-name basis with my family.

I didn't smoke. I changed to skim milk and even *enjoyed* that healthy, vibrant, light-blue tint in my morning cereal bowl. I stayed away from red meat as much as I could. I was married—I had a couple of kids, and I did everything "they" say to keep myself in good shape. But, despite my good intentions, my doctor tells me it was my genes that finally did me in. You know, those little bands of DNA on those squiggly chromosomes that define our hair color, our height, and in my case, exactly where that artery in my heart clogged up.

It all started out innocently enough. One morning, about five minutes into one of my runs, I felt an eerie, diffuse *feeling* in my chest. It wasn't exactly a pain and it certainly wasn't the "elephant on the chest" feeling I had always heard was *the* symptom of a heart attack. When the feeling hit that first time, I considered stopping, but figuring it was only some kind of muscle pull. I decided to just run through it. After all, being fifty years old and as active as I had always been, some joint or muscle in my body was usually aching at one time or another. So I just kept going and the feeling went away.

Two days later, I took off again for another run. The "feeling" came at the exact same time it had hit during the previous run. Five minutes in. Right on schedule. *Damn!* This time I stopped. But I still didn't tell anyone.

My excuse was totally lame, of course. We were scheduled for a family trip to West Virginia and I knew if I told my wife about this, that trip would be off. Since my kids were getting older, I figured we only have so many more years for trips like the one we were planning, and I didn't want to miss out on what looked like an opportunity to spend a wonderful week in the woods with my wife, Kathy, and the kids.

I promised myself I wouldn't overdo it on the trip. Right, sure! I only kayaked seven miles down the New River on a white-water rafting trip and went on several arduous hikes during our week in the Blue Ridge Mountains. But because the pain never recurred, I convinced myself that maybe it *was* only a muscle pull and it would go away, never to be felt again. Yeah—and Hoss Cartwright was a ballerina.

After returning from West Virginia, I tried to run once more—a third time. And, just as had happened the last two runs, after five minutes "it" came back, only stronger and more localized than ever. This time the pressure in my chest was followed by a feeling of warmth spreading into my left shoulder and a tingling sensation in my left arm. The tingling thing was what finally did it for me. Time to admit the obvious and call the doctor.

I told Kathy that evening what I had been experiencing. In one breath of emotion, she was all at once infuriated with me that I had kept the situation from her, anxious about where it would lead, and relieved that I was going to call our doctor.

I called Dr. Murray, who was also one of my best friends, that morning, telling him, "Doc, you know, I've been having some exercise-induced chest pains the last few times I ran, and—"

"What do you mean, the last *few* times you ran?!!" Murray interrupted me, more irate by how long I had let this go than with anything else. "How many times has it happened?"

"Oh, about three or four, but—"

"I'll get you into the cardiac lab *today* and we'll get a stress test," he said, sounding more like a scolding parent than the friend I had skied with wearing nothing but shorts and T-shirts a decade ago. But that's another story—actually, several more stories. "I'll call you back." He hung up without waiting for an answer.

His stressing *today* made me uneasy and assured me both at the same time. Murray was taking control and I knew I just had to let him.

By 3:00 p.m. I was in Dr. Murray's office at Weiss Hospital. He walked me over to the cardiac lab and introduced me to Ian Cohen, the cardiac doc he had lined up for me. I had just graduated. I now had my very own cardiologist. Dr. Cohen exuded such confidence that I immediately knew I was in very competent hands.

Something about his mannerisms said, "I'm in charge and you can trust me."

It was a good feeling for a guy who was going to be fooling around with my heart.

They started the stress test. The test, for those of you who have never taken one, is pretty simple. You walk on a treadmill while they slowly increase the speed and incline. As I recall from the last time I took this test, to get to your target heart rate you are pretty much sprinting at full speed up a wall.

This time, I lasted about the same amount of time I had while running the last three times. After five minutes or so, I got the chest pain again. And, as the pain began, whatever information those wavy lines on the scope convey was indicating something amiss to the docs, and they immediately stopped the test.

"You've got some blockage, son," Dr. Cohen said without hesitation. "You probably know what's next."

"Yeah, I've got a good idea," I told him. "More ice cream?" I asked, making one of the bad jokes I'm known for at times like this.

"Not exactly," laughed both Dr. Murray and Dr. Cohen. "But it's close. It's called an angiogram."

So there it was—the "A" word. Another first. I always knew my circulatory system was going to be my weak link. My father had died of a heart attack at age seventy-two, and his father, as the story goes, died of the same cause in his sixties. And I always knew that someday, somewhere, I was going to be having an angiogram. But at fifty? Me? Now?

I called Kathy and explained to her what was going on. Her voice went from an initial exuberant, inquisitive, "How did it go?" to a barely discernible, "Oh," after I answered her question. The whole situation had now taken on a life of its own, and I knew we were in for quite a stressful week. At least, I hoped the stress would only last a week. But I also knew that we were going to get through this thing. There was just no alternative. I was not ready for anything other than enjoying the next fifty years of my life.

They scheduled the big day for Friday. Here I was in what I had considered pretty good shape. Like I said, the Olympics weren't exactly calling, but I could still run faster than my athletic teenaged kids, ski down a mountain with abandon, and sprint from first to third faster than anyone else I knew. The anticipation was awful and, as it turned out, the worst part of the entire experience. I had the next four days to worry about the angiogram.

Kathy and I were pretty loose as we drove to Weiss Hospital that Friday morning. I was in tears as we said good bye to Erin and Daniella. They were very nervous and scared, and it showed. That was really the first time it hit me. There *was* the possibility here I would never see them again.

We got to the hospital a half hour early—maybe that was one of the manifesta-tions that led to the problem in the first place—and checked in. Dr. Cohen came into the prep room and we talked for a while. I especially liked it when he began discussing the risk percentages. Risk percentages? If he started to talk about the Vegas line on the procedure, I decided I was out of there. The angiogram handicapped out okay. He told me there was a "risk factor" of one-thousand-to-one for fatalities during an angio-gram, but I was a little dismayed by how much the odds went down if they progressed to an angioplasty, and an angioplasty was what was planned here.

"Once we start inflating our little balloons," Dr. Cohen explained, "the risk factor goes to one-hundred-to-one."

Whoa! Suddenly the seriousness of this whole procedure was thrown in my face. I'm sure Kathy saw the pall come over me as the doctor just proclaimed that I was ten times more likely to die undergoing the very procedure they hoped to perform than from the risks associated only with the angiogram.

As it was explained to me, they were pretty sure there was some arterial blockage somewhere. Where it was, how many arteries were blocked, and to what extent any one was blocked could only be determined by the angiogram. Hopefully, once they were in there they would find only one or two arteries blocked, and then use the balloon to push whatever was blocking the artery out to the walls and clear the blockage. Until Dr. Cohen made the one-hundred-to-one proclamation, other than the pain from the procedure, the thing I was truly worried about the most was that they would find too many blocked arteries. That, as they explained, would require a full-blown bypass operation within a few days of the test. And, as reluctant as I was to have this angiogram, I certainly didn't want to have my ribs cracked and my veins taken from my leg and reattached onto my heart.

Dr. Murray had also come down from his office and was doing his best to assure us that we would all still be here on Saturday.

Now, I don't recall where I got the notion that an angiogram was only slightly less arduous than a Civil War leg amputation without anesthetic, but somewhere I had heard they were excruciatingly painful. After all, they do insert a "catheter" (that word alone raises some rather disturbing images) into your "groin" (another word that sounds like it's an area of your body, very close to your "loin," which, on me anyway, has always been a very sensitive area). They then wind the catheter up through your arteries until it settles into your coronary arteries. Once the catheter is in place, they discharge dye that is picked up on X-ray. The path of the dye shows the extent that any of the arteries are blocked. Despite everyone's assurances that the procedure was nearly painless, I was not buying it at all.

Hey, maybe that little pain in the chest wasn't so bad, after all, I seriously considered while waiting in the prep room.

Murray saw to it that I had a nice Valium IV for the test so I was at least partially sedated. I kissed my wife a passionate, "I'll-be-back-from-France- *alive*-after-the-war, honey" kiss, and they wheeled me into the Cardiac Cath Lab. Now, before this, the most sophisticated piece of medical equipment I had ever seen was a blood pressure sleeve, but this room looked like something out of *Frankenstein, 2000*. There were monitors and blinking lights everywhere. Sophisticated-appearing scopes were hanging down from every corner of the ceiling and there were gauges, dials, and other equipment packed into every corner of the stark white room. A low hum emanating somewhere from deep in the room reminded me of the sound the Morlocks made in the movie, *The Time Machine*. It did not look like the room where they give kids ice cream after a tonsillectomy.

"Are you sure we're in the right room?" I nervously asked the nurse who took me in. "I mean, they're not transplanting anything here, right?" I tapped my chest.

"No sir," she reassured me. "There's no transplanting going on around here. You should see *that* room," she added with a laugh, picking up on my unsettled state.

Dr. Cohen came in, introduced his partner, Dr. Levin, and after asking whether I would rather have the Rolling Stones or Hendrix playing on the stereo, sat down and immediately started the procedure.

"The Stones are cool," I told them, the Valium slowing my speech down to about ten words per minute. "Just don't play anything from *Let It Bleed!*"

That received a hearty laugh from everyone in the room.

"You're going to feel a little stick," he told me.

Yeah, a little stick. I'd heard that one before, I thought.

Dr. Cohen continued, "We're going to give you some Novocain. That should numb up the groin"—there was that word again— "so you can't feel anything."

Sure, I thought. Not believing him, I braced for the worst. But nothing— *nada.* I can honestly say I didn't even feel the needle with the Novocain go in. And so it went for the entire angiogram and, as I am pleased to announce, the angioplasty. No pain at all. In fact, I've stubbed my toe and found it to be more painful than the entire procedure. Really!

The banter in the room was going strong as they moved the catheter up into position.

"We've got it in now," Dr. Cohen said to Dr. Levin.

"Okay," I said as they continued. As though they needed me to agree.

Everything was moving along, but at some point, despite my sedated state of mind, I noticed that all conversation in the room suddenly stopped. Knowing what I know now, I figure that's when they discovered that my left descending main coronary artery—the one I also later learned was called "the widow maker"—was ninety-seven percent blocked.

Yikes—ninety-seven percent. I remember I got that grade once on a test in fourth grade. And while ninety-seven being so close to one hundred in fourth grade was good, its nearness to what that number signified now was more than a little disconcerting.

And disconcertion was the emotion of the hour. Despite the Valium, when they informed me of the extent of the blockage, all I could think was, "How did *that* happen?"

I didn't need the doctors to tell me what would have happened had that last three percent stopped up. The word that comes to mind is "flatline."

"Okay, Marc. We see the problem, and we're going to drill it out," Dr. Levin exclaimed after telling me about the ninety-seven percent thing.

"You're going to do what?" I asked.

Up to this point, they hadn't really explained this latest bit of twenty-first century miracle to me, but as they maneuvered around to get the drill in place—yes, I said "drill" into place—they explained it all to me.

"We're going to take a tiny rotor up through the catheter and essentially drill out the plaque, suck it out, and balloon the arterial walls back smooth," Dr. Cohen explained as though describing how he was about to vacuum my kitchen floor. "That should get the job done."

I was afraid to revisit the "risk" talk we had engaged in during our pregame talk. I certainly didn't need to hear that we were now down to ten-to-one. But considering that they already had a catheter *inside* my coronary arteries and were, in fact, right up against the blockage that had been causing my chest pain, this was not the point to be turning back or reconsidering.

"Oh...okay—go get it." I said, sounding to my Valium-ed ears more like a cheer-leader than I had intended.

The sound of the motor that was apparently turning the little rotor deep in my chest provided more fuel for that disconcerting feeling. *Yikes, they really are drilling out the artery on my heart!* As I lay there listening to Mick Jagger, I thought I heard him crooning out, "...Heartbreaker..." but in all honesty, the sound of that drill was pretty overpowering.

Probably having something to do with the Valium, and the general surrealistic scene in the entire room, I couldn't tell you whether they were using that drill on me for five minutes or five hours. But eventually, Dr. Cohen proclaimed triumph when he shouted, "We got it, Marc. You are going to be good as new! All we have to do is smooth it all out now and you're out of here. Hold on for a little while longer."

Like I was going somewhere.

They ballooned my artery, finishing the whole procedure in what I later learned was about an hour and a half. While waiting in the Cath Lab to be wheeled out and into my hospital room for the night, Dr. Cohen came up and told me, "Within about a week, that ninety-seven percent would have probably progressed to one-hundred percent, at which time, if you were lucky, you wouldn't merely have had a major heart attack. More than likely you would have just keeled over, dead. You...are...a...very...lucky...man."

At that, I just closed my eyes and tried to gather my thoughts—and all I could really concentrate on was Kathy, Erin, and Daniella. I wasn't going anywhere, other than to a hospital room for the night—not just yet, anyway.

They kept me overnight at Weiss, and other than the guy in the bed next to mine causing a terrible ruckus during the night, everything else associated with the pro-cedure and recovery was uneventful.

Kathy picked me up the next morning, and we drove home to the hugs and whoops of my two kids. I was never more excited in my life to see them. The recovery period was, other than the one night in the hospital, nonexistent. We went out for dinner Saturday night as though nothing had happened.

It's been a week since my angioplasty. It's funny, but considering what could have been, the word "angioplasty" hardly denotes the seriousness of the situation. I've still not had a piece of red meat or anything else remotely associated with fat, cholesterol, or plaque since the procedure, but I'm sure that will change soon. I figured I laughed in the face of death once, so there's no need to spit in its eye—at least, not just yet.

I feel great, but I felt great before, too—other than those episodes while running. The only change I really feel is a loss of whatever semblance of invulnerability I used to have. And maybe that's good, because obviously I'm not. I've even started to exercise again, and this morning I ran for the first time. When I got to that five-minute mark, I was more than a little anxious. But it passed, as did the ten-, fifteen-, and twenty-minute points, until I completed my entire run without any hint of that chest pain.

So, is that it? Any great moral to the story here? Yeah, I guess there are a few simple ones. One, if you feel chest pain, don't go kayaking—go see your Dr. Murray. Two, don't take any of the time you have for granted. And most importantly, don't be worried about having an angiogram. The test is one-hundred percent painless. Now there *is* that odds thing, but...

Scott Minar

The Other Newfoundland

Not many people knew it in 1988, but there was a Jimi Hendrix bar in St. John's, Newfoundland. We were talking with Gren McGonegal, our new friend and a public television producer on the island. Gren is originally from Sault St. Marie, Canada—or as he calls it with high derision, "the Sault!," drawing out the "u" sound in the middle as if it were a sour taste in his mouth. He was telling us how the bar is a singeing tribute to the freakishly great rock and blues guitarist/singer. There is an old-school jukebox filled with Hendrix tunes, and patrons come in every night wearing his signature headband and hippie clothes—a loose Madras-style shirt, bellbottom jeans with some color embroidered or sewn around the bottoms, a few beads circumnavigating neck and wrist. When we walked by the place once, I poked my head inside. It looked exactly like a nice working-class Cleveland bar, the kind I had my first beer in—dark, clean, cool...an ambiance we might call *smoky,* referring to light and feel rather than scent.

Newfoundlanders are exceptional people. Like a great independent British film, think *The Full Monty* or *The Commitments* here, the place is full of surprises, never what you expect. The quirkiness found in Annie Proulx's *The Shipping News* and in the film adaptation of it is pretty much spot on. The place is filled with legends.

My wife, Robin, and I are here for school. She is a graduate student, and I've been offered a year's teaching as a lecturer in basic English—which in this case means classes like Poetry and the Shakespeare Play or Studies in Short Fiction. I teach Shirley Jackson's infamous short piece about human sacrifice, "The Lottery," and these young Newfies are impressive. They are so much better than my American students, the ones I am used to back in Ohio, it is shocking. It turns out there are very real international cultural differences, even in this North American proximity. Though in truth, Newfoundland is hell and gone from the US.

Driving to St. John's from Cleveland might take about five days and includes a sea trip, what they call a "ferry" ride (but nothing like what we might mean by the term) of either twelve or twenty-four hours depending upon which landing one is aiming for. The shorter of the two—which runs between North Sidney, Nova Scotia and Channel-Port aux Basques, Newfoundland—also requires a thirteen-hour car ride between the landing point and St. John's, across the expansive interior of the island, which is about the size of Texas. And this is all *after* we've managed to arrive in northern Nova Scotia.

When I teach "The Lottery" with such apparent success, I remember that this is the place famed for its photos and newsreel footage of people knocking baby seals out with a club. But Joanne Dobbins, daughter of the island's wealthiest business owner and Gren's girlfriend, tells us Newfies are grossly misunderstood by the Green Movement in this regard. "People *eat* seal flipper around here!" she states emphatically. Save a bullet; make your own McDonald's. Seal flipper sandwich we do not try, though we have sampled most Newfoundland dishes, like fish and brewies (pronounced *brews*) and caribou liver pâté. We've heard that seal flipper tastes bad, like fish fat or fish guts, so we avoid it. Some local treats are to be eschewed in this remote place.

Robin and I arrive by jet at St. John's International Airport, lucky to have been redirected during an attempt to board the Air Canada flight to Saint John, New Brunswick—a different place altogether. The landing field is on a plateau of sorts, surrounded by green shale (called Newfoundland shale) and squat, undernourished pine trees. The latter are everywhere, or so we learn later. There are very few hard-woods on Newfoundland, but the island is filled with pines and has a booming forestry industry inland. Those pines near the city here are small because of the rocky ground and the wind.

Wind is something you have to get used to in Newfoundland. I was walking to class once across campus and over a small patch of sidewalk partially iced with the first winter precipitation. The wind caroming and sluicing around the larger university buildings was so strong, it stopped me in my tracks. I literally had to wait a minute for it to calm down in order to move at all. That had never happened to me before and hasn't since then. It is one of St. John's primary lessons: Weather matters here. There's no taking it for granted. It's a constant concern—something to always pay attention to, not so much because it's dangerous, though it can be, but because you need to compensate if you want to get around at all and do so comfortably.

After a failed attempt at renting a small living space (too small in this case), Robin and I land a cozy basement apartment at Marie's, a B&B in the suburb near the university and adjacent to one of St. John's two hospitals. One morning we see off in the distance, near the front of the hospital building, something we can't identify. It's a huge animal, much bigger than a horse, as if someone crossed a Clydesdale with an elephant. It turns out to be a moose, and we recognize it only after thinking things through. As Dorothy puts it, we're not in Kansas anymore. We learn later, though, that there are neither poison ivy nor snakes on the island of Newfoundland. A great compensation. There are mountain lions and even an occasional polar bear drifting down on the ice floes in spring, however. One of these has to be killed a few weeks before we leave Newfoundland. Polar bears see people as food, and the anesthetizing agent in the dart they fired into this one didn't work. It was probably old stock, Gren speculates.

We are having supper at The Blue Door, Gren and Joanne's favorite upscale restaurant on Water Street downtown. St. John's looks a lot like how I imagine San Francisco looked a long time ago: scarlet, yellow, and boat-blue wooden buildings on a steep hillside rolling down to a natural deep-water harbor and a quaint downtown area. Narrower streets than we are used to and smaller buildings as well. Joanne, who grew up here, mentions that no buildings can exceed four or five stories in height, mostly because of the wind, which as I mentioned before is unprecedented as far as mainlanders can understand. Someone tells us the story of the "unsinkable" oil platform, the Ocean Ranger, stationed 186 miles offshore, east of St. John's. The North Atlantic has some of the roughest seas on the planet, and though the platform was built to ride waves as large as 110 feet, it succumbs to those that are a mere sixty-five with winds exceeding one hundred knots—probably because of an accident, a broken window letting seawater through to the interior. Eighty-six people, the crew on that rig, die of drowning caused by hypothermia in winter waters, and there is nothing to be done by the time the choppers arrive the next morning after the storm abates.

After supper, Gren orders shots of Grand Marnier served in snifters heated by pouring boiling water into their interiors and rolling it around the glass before dumping it out and then adding the orange-flavored liqueur. The scent of orange steam coming out of the snifter is very strong, strong enough to clear our sinuses. I am telling Gren about our first day on the island. Robin and I had been hiking around Signal Hill, a magnificent National Historical Site and park near the city and overlooking the North Atlantic. We walk down vertigo-inducing steps cut into the mountainside (these are not hills) to a stunning view of the sea and very tall cliffs dropping straight into the roiling ocean surfaces below. There is a small castle-like structure built at the highest point of Signal Hill, which has had fortifications of various sorts on its summit since the 17th century. There is a plaque set in a low stone wall separating visitors from a shallow slope that leads to a deadly vertiginous drop beyond it. It reads something like, "Guglielmo Marconi sent the first transatlantic wireless signal from this spot." When we are up there, Robin and I watch a small dingy being rowed around the cliffs by a couple of local cod jiggers. For landlubbers like us, it is an unbelievable scene. I ask Gren, "What the hell are they doing out there in that little boat?"

He says, laughing, "That's nothing! I've seen those guys row so far out to sea you can't see them anymore!" Joanne is smiling, though it's hard to imagine what she thinks about conversations like this one from outsiders like us. "And that's not the worst part!" Gren adds, growing more animated as he unfurls his story. "They're all in hip-waders!" A short pause here, "And none of them can swim! But even if they could, they'd drown in about a minute anyway—the water is so cold. But with those things on, if they fall out of the boat, they go straight to the bottom! They're gone!"

I'm stunned silent and look to Joanne for confirmation, which she gives. She tells us that most Newfoundlanders can't swim because the water is too cold and you have to learn in a pool. There aren't a lot of those. I can't tell if she's having us on in what we'd call in Wyoming back in the States a "jackalope" moment. But it sounds real and plausible. Strange and unexpected things happen in Newfoundland.

Robin and I spend a short cab ride in town with an old toothless gentleman who is a real chatterbox. When we get out of his cab, she says "What was he saying?!"

I say, "*I* don't know!"

"But you were laughing and smiling at him the whole time!"

"I was just trying to be polite!" I answer. We didn't understand a word he said, and we rode in his taxi for twenty minutes.

Joanne, when told this story, remarks, "He was probably from around the bay." Newfoundlanders call any fishing village on the coast of the island "around the bay." But she explains that our cab driver is probably a resident of a fishing village full of Scots who haven't changed their dialect of English since the 17th century. It's that kind of place.

Newfoundlanders are remarkably kind and generous. They live, those in St. John's, in an international port of call that is safer than a suburb of Cleveland or any city in the States. When I ask Joanne which parts of town Robin should be careful in after dark, she looks at me like I have three heads. The answer is none. They're all safe. We see a destroyer from the Portuguese Navy in the deep-water harbor downtown. The Basilica of St. John's, the oldest church of that design in North America, has printouts of its history in half a dozen languages on a table in its foyer, including Russian and Japanese. It's a sailor's town. And it's safe. You can buy blackberry preserves from the Ukraine in its grocery stores and find single malt scotches you'll never see in the US on its liquor shelves.

After we've been back in the US for a decade, Robin and I see a special on NBC's *News Today.* It's about an American engineer from Georgia who donated a large sum of money to build a playground at a school in St. Lawrence, Newfoundland. It turns out Lanier Phillips' story is an astonishing one. He was rescued from a wrecked Navy transport near St. Lawrence during World War II. People from the nearby Newfoundland mining town rappelled down sheer cliffs and stepped into the sea to help collect bodies and get the living out of the water onto relatively dry land. The survivors had to be lifted up those same cliffs in order to reach safety. Two hundred sailors died; only 189 survived. Phillips grew up in Georgia in the 1920s and 1930s and was in fear for his life—from rescuers. He had only known cruelty and prejudice at the hands of white people. The Newfoundlander woman washing oil off his body assumed it had gone into his pores. She had never seen a black person before. Yet when he told her who he was, she treated him as no white person he had ever known did—she completely ignored the fact, washed his body, and stayed with him throughout the night until he was rescued in the morning.

It changed his life. He saw hope and goodness, even love, where he had only known cruelty before. He went on to become a civil engineer, the first SONAR tech nician in US Navy history, and a fellow marcher with Martin Luther King in Birmingham.

Once, waking that night in the darkness, he found the woman nursing him in bed, putting an extra blanket around his shoulders and tucking him in. He said to her, "Is this heaven?"

She was surprised, and answered, "No! Why would you think that?"

He never told her, but it was the first time he had ever been touched by a white woman.

I treasure this story because it reminds me of what I learned living there: this is the way the world should be, peaceful and kind. Generous almost to a fault. In December, Newfoundlanders jog in shorts, running past Robin and me shivering in Eskimo jackets from Woolworth's. They are a very tough people. I used to joke that I would never want to go to war with them. They'd outlast us all.

Our friends, Edward and Beth, send us a collection of essays about Newfoundland as a holiday gift: Robert Finch's *The Iambics of Newfoundland.* Finch tells the most marvelous story of a Newfie hitchhiker in the States making his way through the Midwest. He is actually on an interstate highway with his thumb out when he is stopped by state troopers. They explain to him that you can't hitchhike on the highway here. He responds by saying, in that wonderful Newfoundlander accent, and I can't tell you how prototypical this is of the dauntless people we knew there, "Well, I appear to be *doing* it!"

If Newfies think someone is a little slow on the uptake, they will call that person "some stunned," saying "He's some stunned that b'ye!" the last word here meaning "boy" or "guy." They might also say of such a person that he or she is "like the quilt"— meaning, we supposed when we first heard the expression, about as interesting as one to talk with. Instead of cursing, Newfies take oaths. These always begin, Gren explained to us, with the phrase "Holy lord liftin'" and are immediately followed by a series of invectives involving the gruesomeness of Jesus's suffering. An example might be a Newfoundlander hitting his/her thumb with a hammer followed by this: "Holy lord liftin' sweet suffering dyin'-up-on-the-cross bloody Jesus!" At which point, the presumption is the person feels better having gotten it out.

There is so much color on the island, we could never begin to paint it all in story. We can only intimate what we see there and try to sketch some of it on a canvas. But as great as pictures are, what I've learned is that you have to go places yourself sometimes, or you miss it. And you don't want to.

Cyndy Muscatel

Primal Fear

When the charges of sexual misconduct against Donald Trump, Bill O'Reilly, and Bill Cosby began to emerge, it triggered something in me. *Why,* people asked, *would these women come forward after so much time had passed? And how could they even remember the incidents?* I sat at my computer reading these comments, my hands hovering over the keyboard.

I've never talked openly about what happened when I was in my early twenties. I never spoke of it at all until more than twenty years later. We were watching Anita Hill being grilled on television about her testimony against Clarence Thomas.

"Oh, she's just being dramatic," my mother said. "A trustworthy man wouldn't harass a young woman like that."

"It happened to me," I said.

"What?" she said.

"It happened to me when I was teaching at Meany." This time my voice was louder, and my parents and husband turned away from the TV.

"You're kidding," my husband said.

I shook my head.

"Why didn't you say anything then?" he asked.

"I was afraid to. I was afraid you'd kill him." I looked away. "And I was ashamed. I thought maybe it was my fault."

"What the hell happened?" he asked.

I began to tell them.

• • •

It was creepy from the start. At Meany Junior High, the teachers' mailboxes were in the front office. I opened mine one morning—there was a small book of Browning's *Sonnets from the Portuguese* lying on a pile of notices. I picked it up, wondering how it had gotten in my box by mistake. But it wasn't a mistake, and it was only the beginning.

In 1968, we didn't have the phrase "sexual harassment" at our disposal. A new bride, I had been teaching at Edmond S. Meany in Seattle for two years. I was so head over heels in love with my husband, it never entered my mind that someone else might think I'd be attracted to him. So I didn't understand what was happening at first.

My concentration was on my curriculum, my students, and my homelife—all in a state of flux, all in turmoil. When I returned to teach at Meany, the curriculum and the books were the same as they'd been when I'd left for high school in 1960. Seven years later, it wasn't working. The world was changing fast, and I tried to keep up with it in my classroom. *Julius Caesar* is not one of Shakespeare's easier plays to begin with, and it had no relevance to my students. I started to buy books with my own money to try to interest the kids—books by authors like James Baldwin, James Weldon Johnson, and Richard Wright. The books disappeared from my "lending library" at a rapid rate, which I took as a good sign.

As the Civil Rights Movement and Vietnam protests heated up, civil and uncivil disobedience became the rule of the day. Keeping order and keeping the students' attention was a challenge with the constant bomb threats and visits from the SDS and Black Panthers. I shared a classroom with Mr. Miller, my supervising teacher when I student-taught. He was thirty-nine, stocky, with closely cropped black hair and acne-pocked skin.

Before school or after, we'd often be in the classroom at the same time. As head of the English Department, he had an office adjacent to our room, so he was in and out. I'd be at the desk, correcting papers, waiting for my husband to pick me up. Mr. Miller would roam around the room, smoking one cigarette after another. He carried the tin ashtray from his desk around with him as he paced.

"You've been teaching at Meany for a long time," I said one day. "I remember you from when I went here."

He looked a bit pained by my words, but I went on. "Things are so different now, but you've stayed current. How do you reach the kids?"

"Being honest and being in control are good starts," he said. "You're twenty-two and you look like you're the same age as some of the ninth graders. You're going to have to learn to be tougher."

Armed with his advice, I began to develop my own style. It never worked for me to be autocratic—kindness and respect worked better. But I had a steely look that could nail a student from across the room. And developing a curriculum that grabbed the kids' attention made everything easier.

One day, Mr. Miller told me he'd traded in his car for an old hearse. "Gallows humor," he said.

He also told me how unhappy he was at home. His wife was a nurse on the swing shift, so he rarely saw her.

"I just sit around every night by myself and get drunk," he said another day.

I looked up from the spelling tests I was grading. I rarely drank, sometimes at a party on weekends. I couldn't fathom someone drinking during the week.

"Every night?" I asked.

He drew on his cigarette. "Yeah, I drink a couple of bottles of wine."

I was shocked and repulsed. But I also felt sorry for him. He was so nice to me. Several times, he even offered to drive me home when my husband had to stay late at work. I had no experience with the kind of lonely alienation Mr. Miller described. In a lot of ways, I was still a sheltered kid. I'd gone from my parents' home straight to married life in our studio apartment.

My homelife was filled with love, but it was no picnic either. My husband and I were still learning how to share space and time together. It wasn't always easy. Then my father-in-law dropped dead of a heart attack on a downtown Seattle street. My husband was in a terrible state of grief—he never got to say goodbye to the dad he loved so much. He also had to become head of the family while he worked on creating a career for himself. His family was a mess before his father died. It only got worse.

I had a lot to cope with when I found the book of poetry, so I didn't think much about it. I put it on a table in the office, figuring whoever had misplaced it would find it there. A tiny part of me went on alert, but I ignored my intuition. Three weeks later, I felt sure I'd been silly to feel any alarm. The book had remained on the table for quite some time, but now it was gone. So, no worries!

That's when I received the first note. It sat on top of the book, which was again in my box.

Why did you leave the love sonnets on the table? They are for you, the note said. *They are about us.*

I remember looking around after I opened the note. I felt those prickles of unease they talk about on the back of my neck. Who had written the note? Was he watching me? I threw the note in the trash, returned the book to the table, and hurried out of the office.

The second note arrived two weeks later. It was more explicit. *I'm angry that you didn't keep the book! It's yours. You are so beautiful. I want to run my hand down your leg.*

I can't express how much those words scared me. Looking back, I know it was an elemental fear—an almost primal response. I'd been trying so hard to ignore the weirdness, thinking if I did, it would all go away. From my core, I admitted that wasn't the case. And I just didn't get it. I was no femme fatale. I dressed like a schoolteacher in nondescript, loose-fitting dresses that came three inches below my knee. I wore no makeup and rarely bothered with my hair. What could be my allure?

When my husband picked me up that night, I was silent on the drive home. I felt sick inside—I didn't know what to do. My thoughts churned while I fixed dinner. My husband was so caught up in a basketball game on TV that I don't think he noticed I was so quiet. He fell asleep easily, but I couldn't. I think that's when my lifelong struggle with insomnia began. I felt so anxious, my head whirred with thoughts darting from all directions.

Unwisely, I just kept going as if I'd never seen the book or notes. I told no one, keeping to myself this dark secret. I was afraid to tell my husband—I didn't know what he'd do. I could have talked to Mr. Miller about it, but he seemed so agitated and hungover all the time, that I didn't. I thought about talking to Sunny, a colleague who was my age and also newly married. But I didn't say anything to her. My friends were all busy starting their careers and marriages, so none of them felt available to confide in. And truthfully, I felt sullied and ashamed. I didn't want anyone to know.

The next note came about a week later: *I know you care for me as much as I care for you.*

What the hell? I almost ran from the office to my classroom. Who was this person, and why wouldn't he leave me alone? Why would he think I cared about him? I began to feel hunted, checking over my shoulder to see if someone was following me.

I'll never forget the final note: *I don't know why you are denying your feelings. We need to talk. We need to make plans. Meet me at 3:30 at the coffee shop on Galer Street.*

My hands shook and I had to sit down on the visitor's chair in the office. This was something I couldn't ignore. Whoever had written the note was obviously delusional. Now I felt as if I were in danger. Who was this person?

The next day I found out. Of course, I didn't go to the coffee shop. That would have been crazy. I barely slept that night, waking in a daze to the clock radio alarm. It was foggy that morning and the heat hadn't come through the registers, so the room was cold when I got to school. I kept my coat on as I sat down at the desk. I still had many papers to correct since I hadn't been able to concentrate the night before.

The door flew open, slamming against the wall. I looked up, startled.

Mr. Miller stormed in, coming up fast to my desk.

"Why didn't you meet me yesterday?" he demanded.

"I don't know what you're talking about."

"Yes, you do. I know you do, because you took the note."

He reached toward me. I still remember his stubby fingers with the bitten nails. I recoiled from his touch.

"How do you know about the note?" I still hadn't put the pieces together.

He gave an exasperated sigh. "You know how. I wrote it."

"What?" I shook my head. "Oh, no, not you."

"Of course it's me." He loomed over the desk. I smelled alcohol on his breath. "It's time we work out how we can be together."

I put my hands out to stop him from getting closer. "What are you talking about?"

"I love you. I want to be with you. And I know you feel the same."

I pulled my coat tighter around me. This whole exchange was bizarre and embarrassing at the same time. "Why would you think that?"

He gave me a knowing smile. "Because of all the time we spend together. And you told me to look at your legs."

"I never said that."

"Oh yes, you did. You told me you had a run in your nylons," he said.

I remembered that. I used support hose because I was on my feet all day. They were so expensive that when I snagged a pair, I lamented it aloud. And he thought I was suggesting he check out my legs? With support hose?

It was the farthest thing from my mind. I saw him as a mentor—someone I could trust. Not a sexual partner. Never!

"I just said how expensive the Hanes support hose are. I didn't mean anything else."

"Oh, now you're denying it."

"There's nothing to deny. I'm so sorry you got the wrong idea."

His face flushed with anger. "You've been leading me on."

"Not at all. I love my husband. Only him. I'd never cheat on him."

He picked up a book on the desk and threw it across the room. I flinched as it hit the wall.

"I don't understand," I finally managed. "You're married too."

"I don't care about her!"

I jumped at his shouted words, then eyed the door. How was I going to get out of there?

I began to cry. His anger faded, but tears filled his eyes too. "I love you," he said. "I can't live without you."

"No, that's not true," I said.

"Yes, it is." He extended his hand to me. I pulled even farther away.

Then the bell rang. The door opened and a student peeked in.

"Is it all right to come in?" he asked.

Thank God, I thought. I stood quickly and went over to him. "Of course, Tim. Class is about to start."

Mr. Miller gave me one beseeching look and left the room.

I didn't see him the rest of the day. I stayed in the teachers' room, smoking and correcting papers until my husband picked me up.

"Is everything okay?" he asked when I got into the car.

"Sure," I said. "Everything's fine." I turned on the radio to KJR—the rock and roll music flooded the car. I closed my eyes and leaned back against the seat.

When I tried to fall asleep that night, it all came back to me. I didn't want to think about what had happened, but I couldn't stop replaying the awful moments in a never-ending loop. I tried to make sense of it, but I couldn't.

I felt sick to my stomach in the morning. Maybe I had the flu? I thought about not going to school, but forced myself to go. Mr. Miller wasn't there. I felt so relieved.

On Monday, he wasn't there either. During my break, the principal called me into his office. Mr. Sheehan had been my ninth-grade English teacher.

"Cynthia, sit down," he said.

I still remember the rain hitting the windows as he looked at me for a long time.

"You twenty-year-olds don't realize how alluring you are to a thirty-nine-year-old man," he finally said.

I gave him a questioning look. "Pardon me?"

"Pat Miller tried to kill himself over the weekend."

"Oh, no."

"Yeah, he drank several bottles of wine and tried to slit his wrists."

"Oh, no," I said again. "Is he okay?"

"His wife found him and called an ambulance. They got him to the hospital in time."

"Well, that's good." I was so out of my depth, I didn't know what to think or say.

He gave me a speculative look. "Do you care about him at all?"

I cringed. "I think of...I thought of him as a great guy. Nothing more."

"I went to see him in the hospital yesterday. He told me everything. He told me he didn't want to live without you."

"Oh, God," I said.

"He told me he knew you felt the same."

"No! Not at all. I didn't know what he was talking about. I didn't know he was sending me those notes. I didn't know anything!"

Mr. Sheehan nodded. "Yeah, I thought as much."

"He's so much older. I thought of him more as a father figure than anything."

Mr. Sheehan sighed. "I can see that. He never had you in class like I did. When I see you, I still think of you as that ninth-grade kid. Which is also a mistake. You have definitely grown up into a very pretty woman."

I thought I would die right there, either of embarrassment or anguish.

"Pat is one of my best friends," he continued. "I should have seen something wasn't right. They say he's had a complete nervous breakdown."

I was horrified. Without knowing, I'd caused all of this. I began to cry.

Mr. Sheehan leaned forward and handed me a Kleenex. "You can't blame yourself. This has been brewing for a while now."

"Will he be okay?" I asked, wiping my eyes.

"I think so. They're going to hospitalize him for a couple of months."

He sighed again. "You go on back to your class now. I just wanted to talk to you—hear your side of things and let you know what was going on."

I stood and walked quickly from his office, not looking back.

Mr. Miller didn't return to school until the beginning of the following year. He only lasted a few weeks. He was broken—he no longer could teach. Even though I felt guilty, I was glad I didn't have to see him again.

•••

Writing about this time in my life has been difficult. My stomach clenches and I can still feel the fear of that morning when he accosted me. I guess this is more a story of his obsession and stalking me than it is of harassment. For many years, even after I was no longer teaching and had two children, I'd see that hearse following me.

William Vernon

No Trespassing Signs

Bogue Sound was almost a mile away, near the end of Bogue Field's only runway at that time, and I wished we could hear it lapping the shoreline. The sound of lapping water has a soothing effect. Pretty much everyone else, all the others on temporary assignment out here, except for a few firemen and cooks, had taken the Navy busses back to Cherry Point and their barracks or homes. Under orders, half of my Launch and Recovery crew also remained. We had to clean and calibrate our recovery gear before Monday.

We'd spent this whole Friday, from dawn to dusk, in fact the entire past workweek, catching planes or standing by for emergency arrests during the frequent touch-and-gos of carrier- and land-based aircraft. The roar and the whine of A-4Ds, F-8Us, and F-4Hs had daily assaulted us despite the Mickey Mouse ears that we'd worn.

Lying on our racks in our 15-man tent, we could hear the thick pine forest on the old airfield humming as if it had absorbed so much noise it was at last expelling it, slowly breathing out, trying to return to its normally calm state. Just as we ourselves were trying to do. The screeching of jet engines enters you like a shot of adrenaline so you can only try to relax while your inner self vibrates with energy. We'd already spent four hours since supper decompressing, self-medicating, playing pinochle and poker, drinking beer. I'd lost eleven dollars, a lot of money to a Lance Corporal E-3. I expected the brass would make me a full corporal in six months, three months before my discharge, to encourage reenlistment. Fat chance of that.

"Fuck this!" Sergeant Beetle Bailey yelled in the darkness. "We got to do something different tomorrow."

Sergeant Travis, the crew chief, said, "Before or after we finish overhauling the engines?"

Bailey said, "It's not an overhaul. It's just a clean-up."

Travis said, "Well, first things first."

Johnson, a PFC, said, "That won't take but a couple hours. I'm getting up and running through the woods before breakfast. We don't know shit about this place, and I want to see what's here."

Bailey said, "Nothing here but trees."

Johnson said, "Bullshit! It was a full-fledged base in World War II. Anybody else want to do a little run?"

Travis said, "I'm sleeping in."

Bailey said, "Me too."

I said, "I'll go. A run might make me feel better."

Bailey said, "You fuckin' Jarhead!"

Back home, I used to get up sometimes in the middle of the night just to walk in our three-acre lawn in the valley. I'd go barefoot so the dew on the grass bathed my feet and I felt like the animals there: rabbits, owls, one time about 10 sandhill cranes blown off course by a storm. Inside our house my mother and two brothers slept. The house I'd helped my father build a year before he died was on the edge of our town and the farmland surrounding it. When a dairy herd of Holsteins in the pasture just across Southwest Street from us mooed, bells on their necks would ring. It wasn't exactly a song, but it was melodic. Maybe the cows kept track of each other that way in the darkness.

There were actually four of us who ran at Bogue that Saturday, though I forget who the other two were. We were exercising, keeping each other company, plunging into the out-of-doors in a way that connected us with it and disconnected us from the mechanical/technical world that controlled our working hours. A familiar trail took us past the mess tent where the cooks were preparing brunch, to the runway, which we ran from one end to the other. Then we took the taxiway off the runway and found in its big northern curve an old trail that cut directly east. It was really grown up. Nobody'd been on it in ages.

Following it was like going back in time. The brush and trees hung into and over the trail so we had to zigzag and bend over sometimes to avoid them. Still they hit us, but softly, patting our backs and arms and legs as if encouraging us to go on. Birds darted out of our way. On the trail-sides appeared patches of pavement and a few stacks of what looked like concrete blocks. They were moss-covered, stained green and brown, without a suggestion of what they'd been used for. Other trails occasionally appeared, faint traces of old wheeled imprints turning off to one side or the other. We stayed in single file because just one man filled the narrow gap in the foliage that Johnson was leading us through. We couldn't see much farther than a few feet beyond ourselves.

But my imagination was alive. I knew this large acreage had once prepared flyers for combat in Europe and the Far East. I did not know that there were nearly 900 acres of it in all. It would have taken a full day of our constant jogging to explore it. Hundreds of sailors and marines had lived out here, but the remnants we saw of their earlier presence were only hints of those lives. Twenty-plus years of natural growth lay over just about everything those men had left. We were in boots, tee shirts, and bloused dungaree trousers, which would have protected our lower limbs, yet making our own path, plunging away through the trees to investigate more thoroughly never occurred to us. The limbs were so thick we'd have had to walk, and there was only so much time available that morning.

It was a leisurely run. We were actually double-timing as learned in boot camp, and that's slower than most jogging. We were stepping flat-footed rather than pushing off for speed on the front of our feet. I imagined the flights of those earlier propeller-driven planes as well as their crews, men or boys who were anticipating combat in the near future. Luckily, we were not under such pressure.

The trail took us into ourselves and eventually out to the beach although we hadn't been aware of curving to the south. From the clearing where we emerged, NO TRESPASSING signs on metal posts ran at regular intervals both ways along the coast, informing intruders from the water that this was US Navy property and federal land. The shoreline bore no other human imprints. The water reached up near the forest so I guessed the tide was high. Across Bogue Sound was Emerald Island, which a few years later would become a popular vacation site. At that time it was uninhabited across from us, although an online satellite map shows me it is covered with cottages now. A few of our crew had been to Emerald Island, the town, but it was southeast of our location and out of sight.

As we stood there gazing out at the bright hazy air over the sound and the island, the thought occurred to me that I was on the edge, and not just the eastern edge of America nor the edge of Bogue Field. I was looking over the edge of my time in the Marine Corps. Only ten more months to go. The edges of my military and my adult civilian life. The edge of last night and this particular day. The edge of new possibilities from which I had to make choices. I'd never live at home with my brothers and mother again. They'd changed, leading their own lives without me.

"Clam," Johnson said, breaking my thoughts, pulling something from the ground and holding it up for us to see, tossing it back to me. "Come on. Let's go back and eat."

The first hundred yards from the beach took us through sand that made this the hardest part of our run. Our boots dug into the sand and the sand gave way and pitched us from side to side, so our feet shifted around and we had to struggle to reach the runway's solid end. Meanwhile, the gritty outer covering of mud and sand dropped off the clam as we sank in, pulled ourselves out, and stepped forward. By the time we reached the food, the clam's dark shell was bare. I pried it with my fingertips but it wouldn't open. I needed a knife.

We washed up, went into the mess tent where the chief cook saw me lay the clam down, asked where I'd gotten it, and took it to Johnson. They conferred for a few minutes and went outside to talk to Travis. I couldn't see what they were doing and didn't really care, sitting down to syrupy pancakes, scrambled eggs, toast, bacon, and coffee. I was not looking forward to work, but at least there'd be no shrill aircraft demanding our attention.

We worked hard after eating, mundane activities absorbing the drudgery of it. Bailey and Travis gathered us together, directed our efforts, and hurried us along. We'd eaten breakfast late, but pushed by the sergeants, we replenished the ethylene glycol in the piston of both arresting gears. We checked the valves and both cables, replacing one cable that was damaged with a new one we uncrated and dragged into position: a huge snake dripping with grease that we wiped off with rags. There were a lot of other jobs, mostly cleanups. Policing the runway and both sides of it was our final job. Around four we finished, Travis inspected, gave his okay, and led us to the headquarters tent, which of course was empty of officers and the higher-ranking noncoms.

Just outside it he stopped, turned, and grinned at us. "Party time!" He went inside and came back out drinking a beer. "Come on. We're going to the beach."

The tide was low now so more beach was exposed than when we'd been there before, but it was not the kind of beach where you'd wade out into the ocean and swim. The cook was there ahead of us, a jeep parked nearby with three 30-gallon garbage cans. These were shiny, galvanized, clean, never used, except for one that was full of beer cans and ice.

Then we were clamming, using the three rakes we used when raking straight lines in the ground around our 15-man tent, readying the area for inspection. These were simple garden rakes with teeth that bit only a few inches into the sand-and-mud beach, but that was deep enough. The clams were everywhere near the surface. More plentiful were scallops, hundreds of them almost as large as the clams. Maybe the old WWII GIs had taken clams when they'd been here, but apparently no one else had clammed here in years.

We took off our boots and socks, trousers and tee shirts, scavenging the shore, wading in water and muck, digging out the bounty of the sea, laughing, drinking beer and carrying on like the kids I imagined we were, like the college kids on spring break frolicking in Florida in the newspaper pictures. Our ignorance prompted fierce debates. We argued about needing a license without knowing what the laws were. We argued about size and catch limits without knowing federal or state restrictions. We argued about whether there was a season for eating the shellfish, whether they were safe to eat.

The cook assured us they'd taste good, not to worry. We more than half-filled two of the new garbage cans with the shellfish, took them back to the mess tent, rinsed them in clean water from the 400-gallon water buffaloes parked there, jeeped them back in boxes to the headquarters tent. Brunch was the only meal being served in the mess tent today and tomorrow, Sunday, so this treat was extra, for us and the cook's crew.

Near the tent's entrance, the cook had two of his garbage cans full of fresh water, which a field kitchen immersible water heater in each was boiling. Gasoline dripped from a circular container above the can, down a pipe, into a cylinder whose enclosed metal body was a circle a bit smaller than the can's diameter. In this cylinder the gasoline burned, heating the water from the bottom of the can up. In steel mesh bags we suspended about thirty of the crustaceans (to use a word none of us then knew) in the water above the heating elements. It only took a few minutes for the clamshells to open. With the cook's go-ahead, we dumped the clams out of their metal bags onto large metal baking sheets laid on the officers' and clerks' desktops, put the next metal bagfuls into the boiling water, and ate the cooked ones as they cooled. The cook had prepared large bowls of homemade cocktail sauce, liquid butter, and other condiments. So we ate them and drank.

The edge of the night and the day again approached, an overlapping of opposites. We were free of restrictions. The heavy grip of those in charge had loosened. A guard on sentry duty at the gate could radio us should the Officer of the Day arrive from Cherry Point to inspect conditions here. Such a visit rarely happened, never on a Saturday, but we could hide the evidence of our party quickly. After dark, we'd be able to hide things more easily.

The evening was nearly gone when we crossed the runway to the viewing stands, which were nothing more than a high school bleacher with four rows of wooden seats on a metal framework. Clear of the trees there, we lounged, drinking beer, watching the treetops lose a red-orange glow from the sun. The gloaming came upon us, the slow dwindling of the light, then full darkness. We retreated into the tent and brought out the cards. Played poker until only four of us remained, then pinochle. The mess we'd made surrounded us: empty shells and empty cans. We'd sleep in and clean up tomorrow. The woods were silent and peaceful.

Ignorance can be a blessed thing. Immersion in the now would be impossible without it. Like that day. We'd blissfully sat on the bleachers where in a month President Kennedy and some of the Joint Chiefs of Staff would sit. Where they'd barely escape catastrophe. The catapult crew's launching of a jet aircraft would throw the 500-pound metal front-wheel sled in a beautiful arc directly across the runway at the VIPs. I, with the launch and recovery crew at rest in company formation on the other side of the runway, watched the heavy weight sail through the air directly at JFK. I'd thought it would hit him. It landed just a few feet short, dug into the sand, created a moment of stunned silence, then pandemonium as helicopters flew in, limousines arrived, and the VIPS escaped. An incident never reported in the news. Maybe this is its first public announcement.

We were also unaware of the impending Cuban Missile Crisis. Our crew would see that young president again at the US Naval Air Station at Key West, Florida, in October. He'd wave to us from his limo. We'd be in a Navy pickup truck that I was driving illegally (without permission, no license), Travis and Johnson seated next to me. Likewise, we'd pass and recognize the carefully guarded center on the base storing nuclear weapons, and we'd witness the Key West beaches lined with US missiles aimed south. Annihilation of the entire world seemed imminent at the time, down there on the very southeastern tip of North America.

Even worse for the guys I was with: the Vietnam War was coming. They were all lifers. Travis and Bailey were on their first reenlistment, the other guys intended to re-up. I've often wondered what became of them during the conflict, which didn't escalate until two years after my discharge. About two years after JFK's death. If we'd known of that war so near in the future, would the knowledge have changed anything? Did the war in fact damage any of the guys? We of course lost touch, friends of convenience, friends passing in the night.

In hindsight now, remembering that day, I'd like to rewrite the ending. Why didn't we stay right there at the beach where we found the crustaceans? We were the young warriors, the Native Americans there on the coast celebrating the world's abundance. We could have boiled our food right there, eaten there on the beach, discarded the shells in a pile the way the Indians did where they ritualized their presence and practices all along the coast. I've since then seen their once-huge mound of shells at Edisto Island's "Spanish Mount" in South Carolina and read about the 3,000 years required to build it. We could have started a Marine Corps pile of discarded seashells and left it as a mark of our earlier presence and love of being there, on the edge of the land and the water.

We could have built a bonfire and danced around it as the Native Americans had done before us just down the coast. We didn't know enough then to do that either, but picture this: ten young men in white skivvy undershorts circling a fire that flared out toward our legs, whirling and yelling, surrounded by the darkness pressing down on our circle.

Contributors

Mary Jo Balistreri has two books of poetry published by Bellowing Ark Press, a chapbook by Tiger's Eye Press. Her new book, *STILL,* will be published by FutureCycle Press in 2018. Mary Jo is widely published both nationally and internationally. She has participated in four panels on poetry in the last six months and has plans for additional readings. She is a founding member of Grave River Poets a poetry outreach for schools, churches, and women's shelters. Please visit her at maryjobalistreripoet.com.

Dave Barrett lives and writes out of Missoula, Montana. His fiction has appeared most recently in *Midwestern Gothic, Gravel* and *Cirque.* Dave has work forthcoming in *Cowboy Jamboree* and *Quarter After Eight.* He teaches writing at Missoula College and is at work on a new novel.

Gershon Ben-Avraham's short stories have recently appeared in *Big Muddy, Broad River Review, Chicago Literati, Gravel, Jellyfish Review, Jewish Literary Journal, Steel Toe Review, Sun Star Review, The Avenue, The Vignette Review, Wild Musette Journal of Music, Mystery and Myth,* and *JewishFiction.net.* His story, "Yoineh Bodek," is targeted for publication in the spring of 2018 by *Image.* His nonfiction has appeared in *Forage and Snapdragon: A Journal of Art & Healing.* Gershon grew up in Jackson, Mississippi, and lives in Be'er Sheva, Israel, with his wife Beth, and Kulfi, the family's collie. He holds an MA in Philosophy (Aesthetics) from Temple University, Philadelphia.

Delaware native, **Nina Bennett**, is the author of *Sound Effects* (2013, Broadkill River Press Key Poetry Series). Her poetry has been nominated for the Best of the Net, and has appeared or is forthcoming in publications that include *I-70 Review, Gargoyle, Reunion: The Dallas Review, The Yale Journal for Humanities in Medicine, Philadelphia Stories,* and *The Broadkill Review.* Awards include the 2014 Northern Liberties Review Poetry Prize, and second place in poetry book category from the Delaware Press Association (2014). Nina is a founding member of the TransCanal Writers (*Five Bridges: A Literary Anthology*).

Roy Bentley is the author of *Starlight Taxi* (Lynx House), which won the Blue Lynx Poetry Prize. Books include *The Trouble with a Short Horse in Montana* (White Pine), which was the winner of the White Pine Press Poetry Prize; *Any One Man* (Bottom Dog); and *Boy in a Boat* (University of Alabama Press), which won the University of Alabama Press Poetry Series. Roy is the recipient of a Creative Writing Fellowship from the NEA, six Ohio Arts Council fellowships, and a Florida Division of Cultural Affairs fellowship. His poems have appeared in *Kentucky Review, Prairie Schooner, The Southern Review, Shenandoah, Blackbird,* and elsewhere.

Guy Biederman began writing in Guatemala while in the Peace Corps and later studied at San Francisco State, where his teaching career began. He lives on a houseboat with his wife, daughter, and two salty cats in Sausalito and teaches low-fat fiction. His work has recently appeared in *Carve, Third Wednesday, daCunha, Gathering Storm Magazine, Exposition Review*'s Flash 405, *Flash Frontier, Panoply, Peeking Cat Poetry,* and *Blue Fifth Review*'s Blue Five Notebook. He prefers to write on matchbooks, found ATM receipts, and parking tickets while waiting for traffic lights to change.

George Bishop's work has appeared in *Cold Mountain Review* and *Border Crossing,* and is forthcoming in *Carolina Review.* He is the author of seven chapbooks, including *Following Myself Home,* which won the 2013 Peter Meinke Prize. Bishop's recent full-length collection, *One Dance,* was published in October 2016 by FutureCycle Press. He attended Rutgers University and now lives in Saint Cloud, FL.

A German-born UK national, **Rose Mary Boehm** lives and works in Lima, Peru. Author of *TANGENTS,* a poetry collection published in the UK in 2010/2011, her work has been widely published in US poetry journals (online and print). She was twice winner of the Goodreads monthly competition; a new poetry collection (*From the Ruhr to Somewhere Near Dresden 1939-1949: A Child's Journey*) has been published by Aldrich Press in May 2016; and another new collection (*Peru Blues*) is about to be published by Kelsay Books.

G. F. Boyer has published poems in a number of journals, including *The Southern Review, Prairie Schooner, RHINO,* and *Heron Tree.* She lives with her wife and their cat in rural Pennsylvania, where she edits and manages the *Clementine Unbound* poetry website, works as a freelance editor, and watches the corn grow.

Alan Catlin has been publishing for five decades in a variety of genres and styles of writing; from the art gallery to the noir corners of the neighborhood bar to the halls of the mental institution where his mother once resided. They all feel like home. His most recent publications are the 2017 Slipstream Chapbook Contest winner, *Blue Velvet,* and a companion volume, *Hollyweird,* from NightBallet Press. FutureCycle Press will publish his full-length book, *Wild Beauty,* in 2018.

Rachel Chalmers is an Australian writer living in San Francisco. She studied literature at the University of Sydney and creative writing at Trinity College, Dublin. Her work has appeared in *Salon, Painted Bride Quarterly, The Marlboro Review, The Penmen Review, Southern California Review,* and elsewhere.

Joan Colby has published widely in journals such as *Poetry, Atlanta Review, South Dakota Review, Gargoyle, Pinyon, Little Patuxent Review, Spillway, Midwestern Gothic,* and others. Awards include two Illinois Arts Council Literary Awards and an Illinois Arts Council Fellowship in Literature. She has published 18 books, including *Selected Poems* from FutureCycle Press, which received the 2013 FutureCycle Poetry Book Prize and *Ribcage* from Glass Lyre Press, which was awarded the 2015 Kithara Book Prize. Three of Joan's poems have been featured on *Verse Daily,* and another is among the winners of the 2016 *Atlanta Review* International Poetry Contest. Her newest books are *Carnival* (FutureCycle Press, 2016), *The Seven Heavenly Virtues* (Kelsay Books, 2017), and *Her Heartsongs* (Presa Press, 2018). Joan is a senior editor of FutureCycle Press. Website: www.joancolby.com. Facebook: Joan Colby. Twitter: poetjm.

William Doreski lives in Peterborough, New Hampshire, in a small house in the woods. He taught at Keene State College for many years, but has now retired to feed the deer and wild turkeys. He has published three critical studies, including *Robert Lowell's Shifting Colors.* His essays, poetry, fiction, and reviews have appeared in many journals and several small-press books. His forthcoming book of poetry is *The Last Concert* (Salmon Press).

Karen George is author of the poetry collection, *Swim Your Way Back* (Dos Madres Press, 2014), and five chapbooks, most recently *The Fire Circle* (Blue Lyra Press, 2016) and an ekphrastic collaborative chapbook, *Frame and Mount the Sky* (Finishing Line Press, 2017). Her work has appeared in *The Adirondack Review, The Louisville Review, America, Naugatuck River Review, Heron Tree,* and *Rogue Agent.* She reviews poetry and interviews poets at *Poetry Matters* (readwritepoetry.blogspot.com) and is co-founder and fiction editor of the journal, *Waypoints* (waypointsmag.com). Her website is karenlgeorge.snack.ws.

Thomas Gillaspy is a Northern California photographer. His photography has been featured in numerous magazines, including the literary journals, *Compose, Portland Review,* and *The Brooklyn Review.*

Beth Gordon is a poet who has been landlocked in St. Louis, Missouri, for 16 years. She received her MFA from American University a long time ago. Her work has recently appeared or will be appearing soon in *Verity La, Calamus Journal, FIVE:2:ONE, Slink Chunk Press, Barzakh, Into the Void, Quail Bell Magazine,* and others.

D. A. Gray is the author of one previous collection of poems, *Overwatch,* Grey Sparrow Press, 2011. His poetry has appeared in *The Sewanee Review, Grey Sparrow Journal, Appalachian Heritage, Kentucky Review, The Good Men Project, Still: The Journal, War, and Literature and the Arts,* among many other journals. FutureCycle Press published his full-length collection, *Contested Terrain* in 2017. Gray recently completed his graduate work at The Sewanee School of Letters and at Texas A&M-Central Texas. A retired soldier and veteran, he writes and lives in Copperas Cove, Texas, with his wife, Gwendolyn.

Hayley Mitchell Haugen holds a Ph.D. in 20th Century American Literature from Ohio University and an MFA in poetry from the University of Washington. She is currently an Associate Professor of English at Ohio University Southern, where she teaches courses in composition, American literature, and creative writing. Her chapbook, *What the Grimm Girl Looks Forward To,* was published by Finishing Line Press (2016), and poems have appeared, or are forthcoming, in *Rattle, Slant, Spillway, Chiron Review,* and many other journals. Her critical work appears in *Proteus, The Body in Medical Culture, On the Literary Nonfiction of Nancy Mairs, Stephen King's Contemporary Classics: Reflections on the Modern Master of Horror,* and elsewhere. She edits *Sheila-Na-Gig online* (sheilanagigblog.com).

Dianna Henning has published in *Naugatuck River Review, Lullwater Review, Red Rock Review, Kentucky Review, Main Street Rag, California Quarterly, Poetry International, Fugue, Clackamas Literary Review, South Dakota Review, Hawai'i Pacific Review,* and *The Seattle Review,* among others. She was a finalist for the Aesthetica Creative Writing Award and was nominated for a Pushcart by *Blue Fifth Review* in December 2015. Henning has taught poetry for many years through California Poets in the Schools. She received several grants from the CAC and the William James Association's Prison Arts Program, which gave her the opportunity to teach poetry at Folsom Prison as well as at other CA prisons. Henning's third poetry book, *Cathedral of the Hand,* was published in 2016 by Finishing Line Press.

Sarah Henry studied with Robert Hass and Louise Gluck at the University of Virginia. Today, she lives near Pittsburgh, where she is retired from a newspaper. Sarah's poems have appeared in the *Pittsburgh Post-Gazette, Pittsburgh Poetry Review, Loyalhanna Review,* and many other journals, including *Soundings East, The Hollins Critic, Midnight Circus, The Camel Saloon, Indiana Voice Journal, and Whatever Our Souls,* as well as six recent anthologies. *CHEAP POP* and *Donut Factory* have also featured her humorous prose. More of her work is forthcoming in the *Fredericksburg Literary and Art Review.*

Mike James has been widely published in magazines throughout the country. His poems have appeared in such places as *Negative Capability, Soundings East, Chiron Review, Laurel Review,* and *Birmingham Poetry Review.* Among his ten poetry collections are *My Favorite Houseguest, Peddler's Blues, The Year We Let the House Fall Down, Elegy in Reverse,* and *Past Due Notices.* He has served as an associate editor of *Kentucky Review,* an associate editor of Autumn House Press, the publisher of Yellow Pepper Press, and the Waneta T. Blake Visiting Professor at the University of Maine, Fort Kent. He makes his home in Chapel Hill, North Carolina.

Seth Jani currently resides in Seattle and is the founder of Seven CirclePress (sevencirclepress.com). His own work has been published widely in such places as *Chiron Review, Pretty Owl Poetry, El Portal, The Hamilton Stone Review, Hawai`i Pacific Review, VAYAVYA, Gingerbread House, Gravel,* and *Zetetic: A Record of Unusual Inquiry.* More about Seth and his work can be found at sethjani.com.

Zeke Jarvis is an Associate Professor at Eureka College, where he edits *ELM.* His work has appeared in *Thrice Fiction, Moon City Review,* and *Pithead Chapel,* among other places. His books include *So Anyway...,* a collection of introductions to poems that don't exist, and the short story collections *In A Family Way* and *Lifelong Learning.* His blog can be found at zekedotjarvis.wordpress.com.

Susan Johnson's poems have recently appeared in *North American Review, The Kerf, 3 Nations Anthology,* and *Blueline.* She teaches writing at UMass Amherst and lives in South Hadley, MA.

Diane Kistner is Director of FutureCycle Press and Editor-in-Chief on the book side. She spends an excessive amount of her time hand-holding and putting out fires.

Susan Knecht received a bachelor's degree in English literature from Bates College and a master's in social work from Simmons College. In 2016, she completed Stanford University's Online Novel Writing Certificate Program. Her first novel, *The Drowning Party,* was accepted into Lit Camp, a juried writer's conference in Northern California. Along with short stories, Susan also writes poetry and narrative nonfiction and she had an essay published in the *Write on Mamas Anthology.*

Jennifer Lagier has published thirteen books, taught with California Poets in the Schools, co-edits the *Homestead Review,* and helps coordinate Monterey Bay Poetry Consortium readings. Her newest books are: *Scene of the Crime* (Evening Street Press), *Harbingers* (Blue Light Press), and *Camille Abroad* and *Like a B Movie* (FutureCycle Press). Website: jlagier.net. Facebook: facebook.com/JenniferLagier.

Marie C Lecrivain is the editor of *poeticdiversity: the litzine of Los Angeles,* author of several volumes of poetry and fiction, and a fledgling jewelry designer. Her work has appeared in *Nonbinary Review, Gargoyle, Orbis, The Los Angeles Review, Spillway,* and many other journals. Her new chapbook, *Fourth Planet From the Sun,* will be published by Rum Razor Press in late 2018.

Stan McCormick is a practicing pathologist living in St. Paul, MN, but grew up on a cattle ranch near Durango, CO. His poetry draws from a childhood spent tagging along with his father, a cowboy and truck driver, and from almost thirty years in the study of cancer and other human diseases. A recent spell as a patient himself afforded an interesting context with which to consider medical intervention as a kind of con-tractual intimacy between two total strangers—hence, the poem, "Hospital Notes: Making Peace with a Bladder Catheter." Stan's scientific writing has appeared in many medical journals; his poetry is in *Minnesota Medicine, Thin Air Magazine, Pilgrimage Magazine,* and *Black Fox Literary Magazine.*

Ramsey Mathews was born in rural Georgia. He has undergraduate degrees from Georgia Tech and Georgia State University. While working in film and television in Los Angeles, he earned a master's in modern dramatic literature from Cal State University Northridge and a Master of Fine Arts in poetry from Cal State University, Long Beach. Ramsey is a PhD candidate in English and Creative Writing at Florida State University, where he teaches poetry, composition, and literature. He serves as Production Editor of *The Southeast Review.* His poetry has appeared in *Boaat Journal, San Pedro River Review,* and *Sagebrush Review,* among others. You can find his photography at ramseymathews.photography or on Twitter (@dramapoet).

Marc Mayer is a 67-year-old former hippie/boomer, current attorney by day/rock 'n' roll guitar player by night, who finds the time to retell humorous episodes of his life story in between his day and night gigs. His writing credits include a small project—rewriting the Bible—because, well, it's a really old book and it needed an update. His book, *The Sixth Book of the Torah,* was published in 2014. The *Deerfield Review,* a local newspaper, also published a story Marc wrote about his efforts to obtain health insurance when Obamacare first hit the markets. He has also written, produced and played all the instruments on six CDs of original music from The Marc Mayer Band.

Scott Minar is Consulting Translations Editor for *Crazyhorse* magazine. His poems and essays have appeared in *Poetry International, The Paris Review, Ninth Letter, Kentucky Review,* and elsewhere. His latest collection of poems is *Cymbalism* (Mammoth Books 2016), of which Sherrod Santos remarks, 'This is a seductive and unflinching book, beautifully rendered.' He is the author or editor of six books and is Professor of English at Ohio University Lancaster.

Michael Minassian's poems have appeared recently in such journals as *The Comstock Review, The Evansville Review, Main Street Rag, San Pedro River Review,* and *Third Wednesday.* He is also a contributing editor for *Verse-Virtual,* an online magazine. Amsterdam Press published a chapbook of his poems, *The Arboriculturist,* in 2010.

Cyndy Muscatel's short stories, poetry, and essays have been published in many literary journals. A former journalist and English teacher, she also writes two blogs. Cyndy teaches fiction writing and memoir in Kona, Hawaii, and is also a speaker and workshop presenter. She is writing a memoir of her years teaching in the inner city of Seattle, and working on *Radio Days,* a collection of stories.

Robert Okaji lives in Texas. He is the author of three chapbook collections, two micro-chapbooks, and a mini-digital chapbook. His work has also appeared or is forthcoming in such publications as *Taos Journal of International Poetry & Art, Crannóg, Reservoir, Otoliths, Shantih, The High Window, Oxidant\Engine,* and elsewhere. Visit Robert's blog at robertokaji.com.

Marlene Olin was born in Brooklyn, raised in Miami, and educated at the University of Michigan. Her short stories have been featured or are forthcoming in publications such as *The Massachusetts Review, upstreet, Arts & Letters, The Saturday Evening Post,* and *American Literary Review*. She is the winner of the 2015 Rick DeMarinis Short Fiction Award, as well as a nominee for both the Pushcart and the Best of the Net prizes.

Martin Ott has published eight books of poetry and fiction, most recently *Lessons in Camouflage* (C&R Press, 2018). His first two poetry collections won the De Novo and Sandeen Prizes. His work has appeared in more than two hundred magazines and fifteen anthologies. The poems in this issue of *Good Works Review* are from his manuscript *Fake News Poems—2017 Year in Review, 52 Weeks, 52 Headlines, 52 Poems.* More at www.martinottwriter.com.

James Owens's most recent collection of poems is *Mortalia* (FutureCycle Press, 2015). His poems, stories, and translations appear widely in literary journals, including *The Fourth River, Kestrel, Tule Review, Poetry Ireland Review,* and *Southword.* He earned an MFA at the University of Alabama and lives in Indiana and northern Ontario.

Elena Petrovic is a high school junior from Lawrence, Kansas. She has previously been published in school and local newspapers, and hopes to continue writing in the future.

After growing up in Seattle, **Alita Pirkopf** attended Middlebury College in Vermont. Later, she received a master's degree in English Literature from the University of Denver. Alita became increasingly interested in feminist interpretations of literature. Eventually, she enrolled in a poetry seminar and poetry became a long-term focus and necessity.

Serena Eve Richardson is a poet, essayist, and singer/songwriter. Her poetry is published in *The Alembic, The Round, Third Wednesday, Verdad,* and *Passages North.* Her poetry is forthcoming in *Juked, The Cape Rock,* and *Pennsylvania English.* She received her BA with a concentration in creative writing from Montclair State University. Her forthcoming album, *Some Imaginings,* features poetry that has been transitioned into songs. Serena enjoys practicing Siljun Dobup, a samurai sword martial art in which she holds a second-degree black belt.

Steven B. Rosenfeld is a retired lawyer who has been writing for over 40 years. His published non-fiction includes the public Advisory Opinions of the NYC Conflicts of Interest Board, which he chaired from 2002 through 2012, and large portions of the *1972 Report of the N.Y. State Commission on Attica,* which was nominated for a National Book Award. Two years ago, Steven began writing short stories, two of which were published in *The City Key* and *Inigo Online* in March 2017. Another, "Amy's Story," received an Honorable Mention in the 2016 Short Story America Prize contest and was published in the September 2017 issue of Jewish Fiction.net. He lives in New York City with his wife, Joan, and their two cats, Orville and Wilbur.

Terry Savoie has had more than 350 poems published in the past three decades in literary journals such as *APR, Ploughshares, Birmingham Poetry Review, Cider Press Review, Poetry,* and *The Iowa Review.* His manuscript, *Reading Sunday,* recently won the Bright Hill Competition and will be published later this year.

Judith Skillman Judith Skillman's most recent book is *Kafka's Shadow,* Deerbrook Editions. Her poems have appeared in *FIELD, Cimarron Review, Shenandoah, The Iowa Review,* and in anthologies including *Nasty Women Poets,* Lost Horse Press. She has been a writer in residence at the Centrum Foundation and is the recipient of a 2017 Washington Trust GAP grant. Visit www.judithskillman.com.

Jan Steckel retired early from the practice of pediatrics because of chronic pain. Her poetry book, *The Horizontal Poet* (Zeitgeist Press, 2011), won a 2012 Lambda Literary Award for Bisexual Nonfiction. Her chapbooks, *Mixing Tracks* (Gertrude Press, 2009) and *The Underwater Hospital* (Zeitgeist Press, 2006), also won awards for LGBT writing. Her creative writing has appeared in *Scholastic Magazine, Yale Medicine, Bellevue Literary Review, BiMagazine, Anything That Moves* and elsewhere. She has won various contests, three Pushcart nominations and a Zeiser Artist's Grant for Women. She lives in Oakland, CA. Find out more at www.jansteckel.com.

Anders M. Svenning was born in New York. He started writing with seriousness at the age of nineteen and has been published in many literary magazines throughout the U.S. and abroad. Some of the most recent include *Dark Gothic Magazine, Adelaide Literary Magazine, and Degenerate Literature.* He is the author of *Nonpareil* (Tule Fog Press) and *50 States Poetry* (Pansophic Press), and has a collection of short stories forthcoming, titled *Verdant Grounds, Subtle Boundaries* (Adelaide Books). Anders lives in Palm City, FL.

Judith Terzi's poems appear in journals and anthologies that include *Caesura, Columbia Journal, Main Street Rag, The Raintown Review, Unsplendid, Wide Awake: Poets of Los Angeles and Beyond,* and *You Are Here: The Journal of Creative Geography.* Her poetry has been nominated for Best of the Web and Net, and included in *Keynotes,* a study guide for the artist-in-residence program at the State Theater New Jersey. *Casbah* and *If You Spot Your Brother Floating By* are her recent chapbooks from Kattywompus Press.

Writing is **Bill Vernon**'s therapy, along with exercising outdoors and doing international folk dances. *Five Star Mysteries* published his novel, *Old Town,* and his poems, stories, and nonfiction have appeared in a variety of magazines and anthol-ogies. Recent publications are in *Sin Fronteras/Writers Without Borders Journal, The Coe Review, Likely Red, The Wagon Magazine, The Wild Musette Journal, Bridge Eight*

Literary Magazine, The Creative Truth, Here Comes Everyone Magazine, The Rain, Party & Disaster Society, Peacock Journal, November Bees, Door is a Jar Magazine, Donut Factory, Clare Literary Journal, Dime Show Review, and *Indiana Voice Journal.*

Stephen John Walker was born in Seattle, WA. As a young man, he explored the wharves around Elliott Bay and Lake Union, gawking at, and sometimes sneaking on board, the multi-masted, derelict lumber schooners awaiting their final voyage to the knacker's yard. He dreamt of running away to the South Pacific or the Caribbean to be a crew member on a copra schooner. Later in life, his work and travels fulfilled those dreams. Stephen's debut novel, *Hotel San Blas: A Caribbean Quest,* a finalist in the 2017 Next Generation Indie Book Awards, is set among the islands along Panama's north coast and Vietnam.

Matt Whelihan is an assistant professor and chair of English at Wilmington University in Delaware. His journalism and fiction work can be found in publications such as *Slice Magazine, Cleveland Scene,* and *Punk Planet.* In May 2017, Matt received an honorable mention in *Glimmer Train*'s Short Story Award for New Writers contest for his story "A Painter's Secret." He lives in the Philadelphia area.

Joel Worford is a senior English major at Longwood University with a concentration in creative writing. Along with short fiction, Joel also writes poetry, plays, and songs, the last of which he performs around his hometown of Richmond, VA. A few of his favorite writers are Etgar Keret, Danzy Senna, and Haruki Murakami. Joel's work often explores topics such as identity, relationships, and the African-American experience in the United States.

Jim Zola has worked in a warehouse, as a security guard, in a bookstore, as a teacher for deaf children, and as a toy designer for Fisher-Price, and is currently a children's librarian. Published in many journals through the years, his publications include a chapbook, *The One Hundred Bones of Weather* (Blue Pitcher Press), and a full-length poetry collection, *What Glorious Possibilities* (Aldrich Press). He currently lives in Greensboro, North Carolina.

About FutureCycle Press

FutureCycle Press is dedicated to publishing lasting English-language poetry books, chapbooks, and anthologies in both print-on-demand and Kindle formats. Founded in 2007 by long-time independent editor/publishers and partners Diane Kistner and Robert S. King, the press incorporated as a nonprofit in 2012. A number of our editors are distinguished poets and writers in their own right, and we have been actively involved in the small press movement going back to the early seventies.

The FutureCycle Poetry Book Prize and honorarium is awarded annually for the best full-length volume of poetry we publish in a calendar year. Introduced in 2013, our Good Works projects are anthologies devoted to issues of universal significance, with all proceeds donated to a related worthy cause. Our Selected Poems series highlights contemporary poets with a substantial body of work to their credit; with this series we strive to resurrect work that has had limited distribution and is now out of print.

We are dedicated to giving all of the authors we publish the care their work deserves, making our catalog of titles the most diverse and distinguished it can be, and paying forward any earnings to fund more great books.

We've learned a few things about independent publishing over the years. We've also evolved a unique, resilient publishing model that allows us to focus mainly on vetting and preserving for posterity the most books of exceptional quality without becoming overwhelmed with bookkeeping and mailing, fundraising activities, or taxing editorial and production "bubbles." To find out more about what we are doing, come see us at futurecycle.org.